A STUDY OF FAITH AND PRACTICE

EPHESIANS

JACKIE HILL PERRY

JASMINE HOLMES

MELISSA KRUGER

Lifeway Press®
Brentwood, Tennessee

Published by Lifeway Press® • © 2024 Jackie Hill Perry, Jasmine Holmes, Melissa Kruger

ISBN: 978-1-0877-9031-2
Item: 005843174
Dewey decimal classification: 227.5
Subject heading: BIBLE. N.T. EPHESIANS--STUDY AND TEACHING \ GOD \ CHRISTIAN LIFE
Unless otherwise noted, Scripture quotations are from the Christian Standard Bible®, Copyright ©2020 by Holman Bible Publishers. Used by permission. Christian Standard Bible® and CSB® are federally registered trademarks of Holman Bible Publishers. Scripture quotations marked (ESV) are from the ESV® Bible (The Holy Bible, English Standard Version®), copyright © 2001 by Crossway, a publishing ministry of Good News Publishers. Used by permission. All rights reserved. The ESV text may not be quoted in any publication made available to the public by a Creative Commons license. The ESV may not be translated in whole or in part into any other language. ESV Text Edition: 2016. Scripture quotations marked (NIV) are taken from the Holy Bible, New International Version®, NIV®. Copyright © 1973, 1978, 1984, 2011 by Biblica, Inc.™ Used by permission of Zondervan. All rights reserved worldwide. www.zondervan.com. The "NIV" and "New International Version" are trademarks registered in the United States Patent and Trademark Office by Biblica, Inc.™

To order additional copies of this resource, write Lifeway Resources Customer Service; 200 Powell Place, Suite 100; Brentwood, TN 37027-7707; FAX order to 615.251.5933; call toll-free 800.458.2772; email orderentry@lifeway.com; or order online at lifeway.com.

Printed in the United States of America

Lifeway Resources
200 Powell Place, Suite 100
Brentwood, TN 37027-7707

Authors represented by Austin Wilson of Wolgemuth & Wilson

Author photos by Andrew Abajian

EDITORIAL TEAM, LIFEWAY WOMEN BIBLE STUDIES

Becky Loyd
Director, Lifeway Women

Tina Boesch
Manager

Chelsea Waack
Production Leader

Laura Magness
Content Editor

Sarah Kilgore
Production Editor

Afiya Anyabwile
Copy Editor

Lauren Ervin
Art Director

TABLE OF CONTENTS

4   ABOUT THE AUTHORS

5   GETTING STARTED

8   SESSION ONE: Introduction

10   SESSION TWO: Praise & Prayer

44   SESSION THREE: Alive & Unified

76   SESSION FOUR: Mystery & Power

110   SESSION FIVE: Unity & Maturity

140   SESSION SIX: Light & Love

172   SESSION SEVEN: Empowered & Equipped

202   ENDNOTES

204   NOTE TAKING PAGES

209   VIDEO REDEMPTION CARD

THE AUTHORS

JACKIE HILL PERRY is a Bible teacher, writer, and artist. She is the author of *Jude: Contending for the Faith in Today's Culture*; *Gay Girl, Good God: The Story of Who I Was, and Who God Has Always Been*; *Holier Than Thou: How God's Holiness Helps Us Trust Him*; and *Upon Waking: 60 Daily Reflections to Discover Ourselves and the God We Were Made For*. At home she is known as wife to Preston and mommy to Eden, Autumn, Sage, and August.

JASMINE HOLMES is the author of *Never Cast Out: How the Gospel Puts an End to the Story of Shame*; *Carved in Ebony: Lessons from the Black Women Who Shape Us*; and *Mother to Son: Letters to a Black Boy on Identity and Hope*. She is also a contributing author for several books and a frequent contributor for *The Gospel Coalition*, *Desiring God*, *Christianity Today*, and more. She and her husband Phillip are parenting their children in Jackson, Mississippi.

MELISSA KRUGER serves as vice president of discipleship programming for The Gospel Coalition (TGC). She's the author of multiple books, including *The Envy of Eve: Finding Contentment in a Covetous World*; *Walking with God in the Season of Motherhood*; *Growing Together: Taking Mentoring Beyond Small Talk and Prayer Requests*, and *Wherever You Go, I Want You to Know*. Her husband, Mike, is the president of Reformed Theological Seminary and they have three children.

GETTING STARTED

Because we believe discipleship happens best in community, we encourage you to do this study with other women at your church or in a group setting. Or, consider enlisting a friend or two to go through it with you. This will give you study friends to pray with and connect with over coffee or through text or email so you can chat about what you're learning.

PERSONAL STUDY

Each week features five days of personal study that walk you verse-by-verse through Ephesians. You'll find questions to help you understand and apply the text, plus insightful commentary to clarify your study.

WATCH & DISCUSS

At the end of each week you'll find pages that provide space for you to take notes during the videos and follow along with your small group discussion.

DIGGING DEEPER

Included throughout the study are a few pages of extra reading to help broaden your understanding of Paul's original audience and the cultural context for Ephesians.

Extra Resources

Scan me

LEADER GUIDE

A free leader guide PDF is available for download at **lifeway.com/ephesiansstudy**. The leader guide offers several tips and helps along with discussion guides for each session.

BACKGROUND ON THE LETTER TO THE EPHESIANS

AUTHOR: Paul the apostle (1:1)

DATE: About AD 61

BIG PICTURE

In God's eternal plan, God's great masterpiece, the church, has now been manifested. Christ is united with all the redeemed, whether Jew or Gentile, transforming relationships in this life and leading to a glorious future.

SUMMARY

Ephesians is written by the apostle Paul to the church in the city of Ephesus. Paul spent three years among the Ephesians, but this letter is written about 7–8 years after his time there. His letter divides into two parts: Chapters 1–3 are doctrinal and chapters 4–6 are practical. There are no imperatives in chapters 1–3, everything is descriptive, but chapters 4–6 are filled with directives telling believers how to conduct themselves in keeping with their calling.

Paul began his letter with thankfulness as he shared with his readers about God's redemptive work in salvation (1:3-14). He wanted them to know the power available to them through Christ (1:15-19) and he reminded them that this power comes to persons who were dead in sin but saved by grace (2:1-10). In Christ, both Jews and Gentiles are reconciled to God and to each other and are joined together in the church (2:11–3:21).

In the second half of the letter, Paul explained how our beliefs transform how we live. He focused specifically on how our faith impacts our church life, personal life, and family life. To conclude his letter Paul called his readers to put on God's armor to avoid Satan's temptations and to triumph over his attacks (4:1–6:24).[1]

PLACES IN EPHESIANS ▶

This map highlights some of the key places from Paul's third missionary journey in and around Ephesus.

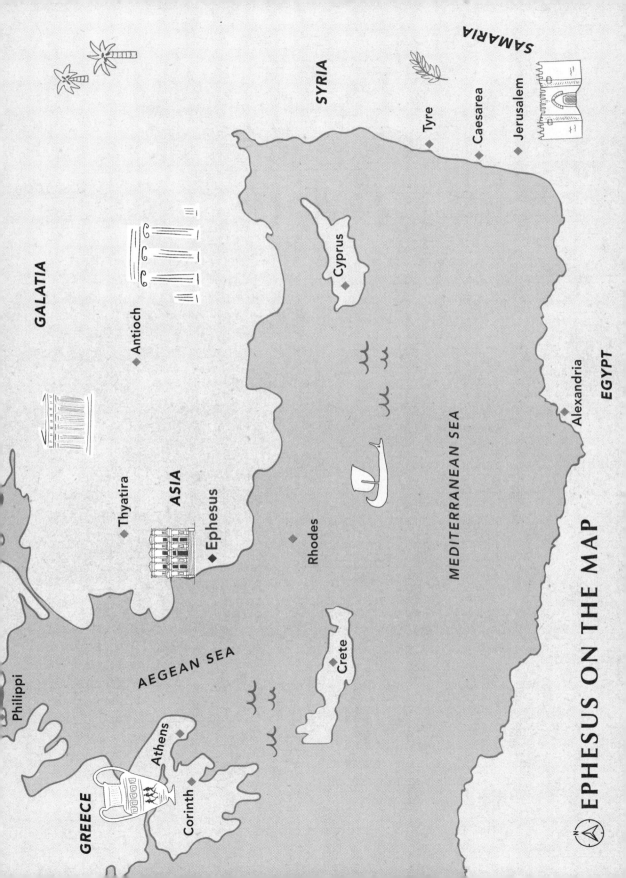

EPHESUS ON THE MAP

INTRODUCTION

The book of Ephesians is often known for the individual themes it addresses. Within the six brief chapters of this letter, we encounter some of the most famous New Testament passages on topics such as God's work in salvation; unity and diversity in the body of Christ; Jesus as the cornerstone; spiritual gifts; submission; familial relationships; and the need to prepare for spiritual battle by putting on the full armor of God.

Like all of Scripture, though, this book of the Bible was never meant to be parsed out into excerpts, disconnected from the full context. When Paul wrote Ephesians, he wrote a single letter to a specific church full of real saints. Everything from his opening greeting to his run on sentences and intercessory prayers was crafted within a theological framework that he ordered with intentionality and care. And it's with this same carefulness that we should read it as recipients today.

As we study Ephesians, it's tempting to get lost in the trees and miss the forest. There are so many beautiful individual truths to explore, but we also want to see the larger picture of God's purposefulness and goodness as we consider the entire epistle. The first half of Paul's letter reveals God's loving pursuit of His adopted children, as well as the abundant riches of our spiritual blessings. In these chapters we read one of the clearest presentations of the gospel in all of Scripture, along with Paul's heartfelt prayers for the spiritual health of the church. Then with chapter 4, Paul makes a clear transition to faith in practice. As saints who have been transformed from death to life through Jesus Christ, how now do we live? What virtues and characteristics should be evident in our daily lives? How do we relate to one another with love? How do we live out of the abundant grace and mercy God has showered on us? And how do we fight the battle of faith while we wait for Jesus to return?

As we study verse-by-verse through this letter together, we hope you'll walk away with a deeper understanding of your merciful and forgiving Father, as well as your calling as His beloved and adopted saint. As you increasingly understand the riches of His kindness, we pray that you'll walk in a manner worthy of your calling—to the praise of His glorious grace.

WATCH & DISCUSS

*Watch the Session One video. Discuss the following questions with your Bible study group. A more extensive leader guide is available for free download at **lifeway.com/ephesiansstudy**.*

1 Going into your Ephesians study, what is one thing you know about this book of the Bible? It could be anything from a key teaching or famous verse, to who wrote it or why.

2 After watching the introduction video, what excites you about studying Ephesians? What do you hope to learn about who God is and who you are in Him?

3 Jackie describes Bible interpretation as a community project. What are some ways we can encourage, challenge, and hold one another accountable as we go through this study?

4 What is one thing you will ask God to do as He works in you through this study?

To access the video sessions, use the instructions in
the back of your Bible study book.

PRAISE & PRAYER

A friend once emailed me asking for children's movie or book recommendations that don't have orphan themes. She'd recently adopted two siblings from foster care and wanted movies that didn't remind them of their loss. The more I pondered her question, I was surprised at how many came to mind involving orphans: movies like *Bambi*, *Cinderella*, *Frozen*, *The Jungle Book*; or characters like Anne of Green Gables, Oliver Twist, the Boxcar Children, and of modern-day fame, Harry Potter. Orphans are everywhere in children's stories.

This made me stop and consider, *Why are we so attracted to these tragic tales?* Whether we've lost a parent or not, we all resonate with a child who's rescued from the loneliness of an orphanage and finds her forever family. And whether we were brought up in loving homes or difficult homes, we've all experienced the brokenness of home. Even in our belonging we find ourselves longing to belong. We may know our own name, but we're not quite sure how to answer the question, *Who am I?*

Fictional stories in literature often represent our deepest longings and fears because they echo a bigger story—the one true story that's being told on the pages of Scripture and in your life and mine. As you read Ephesians over the next several weeks, don't miss the drama. Paul pulls back the curtain and reveals orphans being adopted with heavenly inheritances, cosmic powers engaged in spiritual combat, the sacrificial love between a Husband and His bride, and the rightful King who is seated on an eternal throne. It makes me want to grab some popcorn and prepare for the show. However, this experience is so much more than entertainment. Rather than lose ourselves in someone else's story, we find ourselves in the Bible's story. God's Word is an invitation to life. And each of us has a glorious part to play. I hope you're excited. I know I am. Let's begin.

Melissa

EPHESIANS 1

GREETING

[1]Paul, an apostle of Christ Jesus by God's will:
To the faithful saints in Christ Jesus at Ephesus.
[2]Grace to you and peace from God our Father and the Lord Jesus Christ.

GOD'S RICH BLESSINGS

[3]Blessed is the God and Father of our Lord Jesus Christ, who has blessed us with every spiritual blessing in the heavens in Christ. [4]For he chose us in him, before the foundation of the world, to be holy and blameless in love before him. [5]He predestined us to be adopted as sons through Jesus Christ for himself, according to the good pleasure of his will, [6]to the praise of his glorious grace that he lavished on us in the Beloved One. [7]In him we have redemption through his blood, the forgiveness of our trespasses, according to the riches of his grace [8]that he richly poured out on us with all wisdom and understanding. [9]He made known to us the mystery of his will, according to his good pleasure that he purposed in Christ [10]as a plan for the right time — to bring everything together in Christ, both things in heaven and things on earth in him.

[11]In him we have also received an inheritance, because we were predestined according to the plan of the one who works out everything in agreement with the purpose of his will, [12]so that we who had already put our hope in Christ might bring praise to his glory.

[13]In him you also were sealed with the promised Holy Spirit when you heard the word of truth, the gospel of your salvation, and when you believed. [14]The Holy Spirit is the down payment of our inheritance, until the redemption of the possession, to the praise of his glory.

PRAYER FOR SPIRITUAL INSIGHT

[15]This is why, since I heard about your faith in the Lord Jesus and your love for all the saints, [16]I never stop giving thanks for you as I remember you in my prayers. [17]I pray that the God of our Lord Jesus Christ, the glorious Father, would give you the Spirit of wisdom and revelation in the knowledge of him. [18]I pray that the eyes of your heart may be enlightened so that you may know what is the hope of his calling, what is the wealth of his glorious inheritance in the saints, [19]and what is the immeasurable greatness of his power toward us who believe, according to the mighty working of his strength.

GOD'S POWER IN CHRIST

[20]He exercised this power in Christ by raising him from the dead and seating him at his right hand in the heavens — [21]far above every ruler and authority, power and dominion, and every title given, not only in this age but also in the one to come. [22]And he subjected everything under his feet and appointed him as head over everything for the church, [23]which is his body, the fullness of the one who fills all things in every way.

1

EPHESIANS 1:1-2

Memory Verse:

Blessed is the God
and Father of our
Lord Jesus Christ,
who has blessed us
with every spiritual
blessing in the
heavens in Christ.

Ephesians 1:3

YOU'VE GOT MAIL

**Begin by reading or listening to the
entire letter to the Ephesians.**

It's six chapters and should take you about twenty minutes. If
you don't have time to read the entire letter right now, listen
to it later today while you go on a walk, ride in your car, or are
doing chores around the house.

At this point in my life, I receive a lot of uninteresting mail.
From the packaging alone, I can easily sort my stack of
envelopes between bills to pay and junk mail to toss. That's
why I'm always excited to see a hand-addressed letter with
a familiar name in the corner. In a world of impersonal
greetings and various requests, it's wonderful to receive mail
from a friend.

The letter to the Ephesians was written by the apostle Paul
to the Christians in the city of Ephesus. As we begin our
study, it's helpful to remember that these are real historical
figures, living in a particular cultural context. These are words
between believers, meant to encourage both their faith in
Jesus and their practice (living out) of that faith.

Now return to Ephesians 1 and read verses 1-2 (p.12).

1. **How does Paul identify himself at the beginning of
   this letter?**

2. **Read Ephesians 3:1 and 4:1 also. What do you learn
   from these passages about Paul's current situation as he
   writes this letter?**

Our study begins where the letter begins—by identifying its author. Paul describes himself as an apostle—by God's will. It's important to note that Paul didn't choose this position of authority for himself. Rather, God appointed him for this role when He appeared to Paul in a blinding light on the road to Damascus (Acts 9:1-16).

In addition to describing himself as an apostle, Paul referred to himself as "the prisoner of Christ Jesus on behalf of you Gentiles" (3:1) and "the prisoner in the Lord" (4:1). Paul wasn't speaking figuratively here; he was imprisoned for his service to the Lord and wrote many of his New Testament letters while under Roman guard (Acts 28).

3. **Read 1 Corinthians 15:9-11. How did Paul describe himself in these verses? What did he mean that he persecuted the church of God? (See Acts 9:1-19 for more of Paul's background. In these verses he's referred to by his Hebrew name,** *Saul. Paul* **is his Greek name.)**

Don't miss the irony here—one of the greatest persecutors of the early church wrote Ephesians as a prisoner for the gospel. Meeting Jesus transformed Paul's life, and he became one of Christianity's greatest missionaries. In his own words, "I intensely persecuted God's church and tried to destroy it . . . But when God, who from my mother's womb set me apart and called me by his grace, was pleased to reveal his Son in me, so that I could preach him among the Gentiles . . ." (Gal. 1:13-16). This transforming power of the gospel is one of the themes we'll see in the early pages of Ephesians.

4. **Read 1 Corinthians 14:37 and 1 Thessalonians 2:13. What did Paul understand about his authority as an apostle?**

Paul's words weren't just his opinions. Like Moses and the prophets before him, he wrote under the inspiration of the Holy Spirit. His words were written at a particular time to a particular church, but they are intended for all Christians for all time.

As we read the book of Ephesians, I hope you'll be encouraged (and maybe a little surprised) by how relevant Paul's words are to you in your life today. Just as in creation, God speaks and life bursts forth. As we read and study God's Word, it's life-giving. These words are powerful, not because they're the words of Paul, but because they're breathed out by God (2 Tim. 3:16).

5. Before we get too far along, it's also helpful to know a little bit about the letter's recipients. How does Paul address the Ephesians at the beginning of this letter? Is that identification surprising to you? Why or why not?

Paul visited Ephesus on his third missionary journey, and Luke records the highlights of his time there in Acts 19.

6. Read Acts 19. Note what you learn about the following:

   ◆ Jewish response to Paul's message (see 19:8-9)

   ◆ Time spent in Ephesus (see also Acts 20:31)

   ◆ Religious background of the Ephesians

7. Now read Acts 20:17-38. What else do you learn about Paul's ministry among the Ephesians from this passage?

These passages from Acts help put into context Paul's ministry among the Ephesians. Even though his initial greetings may seem impersonal, Paul spent three years with them. During those years his teaching was met with a wide variety of responses, as we see in Acts 19. Most likely he wrote this letter to them during the time of his imprisonment in Rome, which sets this letter about 7–8 years after his time in Ephesus.

Ephesus was a port city on the west coast of Asia (part of modern-day Turkey), where one could find a variety of religious practices. The presence of a synagogue meant that it was home to a number of Jewish families. The culture was inundated with idolatry, reliant upon magical arts, and curious about demons. At the center of religious life was the worship of Artemis, whose temple was located in Ephesus and was one of the Seven Wonders of the ancient world. Additionally, the worship of the emperor and his family was a prominent feature of life. Imagery of emperors as warrior gods appeared on coins and altars throughout the city.[1]

8. **Paul's first words to these Ephesian saints were "grace" and "peace," which is a standard part of Paul's greeting in all of his New Testament letters. Look up the following words in a standard English dictionary, and write the definitions below.**

GRACE

PEACE

Why do you think these two terms were Paul's chosen way to begin his letters?

As Paul wrote this letter, he understood the cultural practices and religious tensions of the Ephesians. The gospel—the good news of grace and peace freely given through Christ—was an unwelcome religious message for many who profited off magic arts and idolatry. It was most likely difficult to be a Christian in this hostile culture, so Paul's initial address to the "faithful saints" offering "grace to you and peace from God our Father and our Lord Jesus Christ" would have been an encouraging and welcome greeting.

You may not feel like much of a saint some days (nor do I!), but it's the biblical identification of the people of God. It's not a name for the super spiritual or theologically trained. It's the name of everyone who by faith believes in Jesus. In our next lesson, we'll explore more of what that means, but for today, take a little time to let that identity sink into your soul. The question *Who am I?* has its first hint of an answer: *I'm a saint!*

Knowing who we are matters. When we try to earn our relationship with God by working harder, it leaves us exhausted and weary. And no matter how hard we try, we can never be good enough to earn the identity of a saint. It's a name that's given to us—just like Paul was given the title of apostle. Yes, we still struggle with sin, but by faith in Christ, we can rest assured that God greets us with grace and peace and considers us His saints.

Reflect

Today, as you go about your day, remember that you are a beloved saint. And God invites you to cast all your burdens on him because he cares about you (1 Pet. 5:7). Spend some time in prayer thanking Him for the grace and peace that are freely yours in Christ. Ask Him to help you live joyfully as a saint, set apart by Him and for Him.

ONE REALLY LONG SENTENCE

Read Ephesians 1.

EPHESIANS 1:3-14

Have you ever written something and, upon re-reading it, realized, *Wow, that was a really long and complex sentence*? Or perhaps you've experienced sending a "quick" voice messaging a friend, and suddenly you're at the ten-minute mark? I know I'm guilty of both!

Memory Verse:

Blessed is the God and Father of our Lord Jesus Christ, who has blessed us with every spiritual blessing in the heavens in Christ. *Ephesians 1:3*

The passage we're studying today and tomorrow has a similar feel to it. Paul began his letter to the Ephesians with the longest sentence in any of his epistles. In our English translations, verses 3-14 are broken up into multiple sentences. But in the original Greek this entire passage is one long sentence. As commentator John Stott notes, "His speech pours out of his mouth in a continuous cascade. He neither pauses for breath, nor punctuates his words with full stops."[2]

Today we'll spend some time observing what's in the text, and then tomorrow we'll consider how to interpret what it means and apply it to our lives. We'll follow this same pattern (observe one day, then interpret and apply the next) throughout our study of the first two chapters of Ephesians.

Now read Ephesians 1:3-14.

9. **When someone talks without pausing to take a breath, usually they're pretty excited about something. Who (and what) is Paul so excited to talk to the Ephesians about?**

10. **Paul begins his letter to the Ephesians with a benediction or praise of all that God has done on our behalf. List out every verb in this passage describing what God has done for His people.**

Example: God **blessed** us with every spiritual blessing (v. 3)

11. **Look up the following words in a standard English dictionary. What do you learn?**

PREDESTINED (V. 5)	
REDEMPTION (V. 7)	
SEAL/SEALED (V. 13)	

Paul is clear from the beginning of his letter that God is at work in our lives and in the world. These three terms point to God's past, present, and future work. Before the foundation of the world, God had a plan for redemption. He was thinking about you and me long before we were even born. If that's difficult for you to wrap your mind around, it is for me too! And it's a good reminder that God's ways are beyond our comprehension. While we may not always understand the ways God is at work, we can rest assured that He has a plan. He is active in our lives now and forever.

12. **Go back through this passage (pp. 12-13) and underline every time you see the words "according to." List out each of these phrases by writing out "according to X." (Hint: you should find it four times.)**

13. Now (circle) each occurrence of the words *predestined* and *purposed*.

14. As you read this passage, consider the following questions about our salvation:

   ◆   Who blessed us with salvation?

   ◆   When did He choose us?

   ◆   For what purpose did He choose us?

   ◆   Why did He adopt us?

   ◆   How did He save us? (see 1:7-9)

It's clear as we read this passage that Paul is overwhelmed by the glorious good news of the gospel. From before the foundation of the world, God our heavenly Father chose us to be holy and blameless in love before Him. He redeemed us through the sacrificial death and resurrection of Jesus, and He seals us forever through the power of the Holy Spirit. Paul's words in this passage may leave you with some questions, but what's clear is that our adoption into God's family is *according to His good pleasure*, not according to our being good enough.

15. What does it mean to be adopted? Why is this a fitting term?

Adoption in the Roman Empire came with full privileges of name, estate, and inheritance. And according to Jewish law, the firstborn son in Israel received a double inheritance (Deut. 21:15-17). So, when Paul writes that we're "adopted as sons," he's in no way excluding adopted daughters. It means that both men and women receive the firstborn son privileges of name (saint), estate (in Christ), and inheritance (eternal life with Christ).

16. **As you consider words like "predestined," "chosen," and "according to his plan or will," what is confusing or uncomfortable? What is hopeful or encouraging?**

17. **Read Hebrews 9:22. How does this passage help you understand what Paul means by the following phrases: "redemption through his blood" and "the forgiveness of our trespasses"? How do those two concepts go together?**

18. **How do we gain forgiveness? What did Jesus do so that we might be redeemed?**

Sin is serious. When the first humans sinned, their action broke the perfect relationship they had with God and with each other (Gen. 3). Because God is gracious and desires relationship with His children, He created a way for their relationship with Him to be restored. However, this restoration came with a cost. God's goodness and justice prevents Him from ignoring sin, so He made a way for forgiveness that maintained His justice and righteousness. Leviticus 17:11 tells us, "For the life of a creature is in the blood, and I have appointed it to you to make atonement on the altar for your lives, since it is the lifeblood that makes atonement." The author of Hebrews helps us see how the Old Testament animal sacrifices pointed forward to the ultimate and necessary (Heb. 10:4) sacrifice for sin—the death of Jesus, the very Son of God.

19. What is the down payment of our inheritance? What do you think that means about our full inheritance?

20. Throughout our study of Ephesians, we want to pay attention to Paul's frequent mentions of all three Persons of the Trinity. Reflect on what Ephesians 1:3-14 reveals about:

God the Father	God the Son	God the Spirit

Reflect ——————————————————————————————

In one sentence, Paul has given us a full overview of the lavish riches that are ours in Christ. We'll dig deeper into the implications for our lives tomorrow, but for today, take a few minutes to write out your own benediction of praise to God.

Thank Him for the way He has saved you and how He continually works in your life today. Spend time throughout the day savoring these truths and reminding yourself:

I am a saint.
I am adopted, redeemed, and forgiven.
I have an inheritance coming.

DAY THREE

3

EPHESIANS 1:3-14

Memory Verse:

Blessed is the God
and Father of our
Lord Jesus Christ,
who has blessed us
with every spiritual
blessing in the
heavens in Christ.
Ephesians 1:3

HEAPED UP HAPPINESS

Begin today by reading through Ephesians 1 again.

If you have another Bible translation available, I encourage you
to read it in a different version. I've found that sometimes the
slight differences make me notice the details of the passage in a
new way. Biblegateway.com is a helpful website for this.

Now that we've spent some time observing the text, today
we'll consider how to interpret what it means and apply it to
our lives. It's one thing to list out everything God has done
for us; it's another thing to understand the riches of those
blessings; and it's another thing still to live in light of those
truths. We want our observations to lead to understanding
and our understanding to lead to transformation.

21. Now reread Ephesians 1:3-14. What does it mean
    that we've been blessed with every spiritual blessing in
    the heavens? What's the difference between spiritual
    blessings and earthly blessings?

We tend to think of blessings as things that make our lives
easier—health, money, relationships, and so on. While all of
these can be blessings in our lives, they pale in comparison
to the spiritual blessings we have in Christ. Ultimately, every
earthly blessing we possess is temporary. In contrast, our
spiritual blessings are fully secure and can never spoil or fade.

Consider how one theologian reflects on this passage:

> *In this majestic section, Paul wrote of the blessings that
> belong to the church through the Father, Son, and Holy
> Spirit. . . . These blessings include our union with Christ;
> being seated with him in the heavenlies; and our adoption,
> redemption, and election. All spiritual gifts and service
> abilities also flow out of these spiritual blessings that God
> gives to every believer at the time of salvation.*[3]

22. Think about what you most often thank God for in your life. In what ways do we often focus on our earthly blessings instead of our spiritual blessings? Why do you think we do this?

23. In light of Paul's circumstances (Eph. 3:1; 4:1), what is surprising about how he begins this letter? What can you learn from Paul's example when faced with unwanted circumstances in your own life?

Because Paul's eternal future was secure, he knew his hardships were temporary. He might have been in prison then, but one day, he would be in glory! Future hope gives us present joy, even when our circumstances are difficult and painful.

24. Read through this passage one more time. Look for the following, and highlight each in a different way in the text:

◆ What happened in the past for our salvation?

◆ What is true in the present about our salvation?

◆ What hope is a future aspect of our salvation?

Theologians will often discuss our salvation in past, present, and future terms. We are saved (justification), we are being saved (sanctification), and one day we will finally be saved (glorification).

Justification: God redeemed us by Christ's blood and adopted us as children. His justification means we are fully free from sin's penalty.

Sanctification: The Holy Spirit lives inside us presently, continually at work to make us holy. Present grace frees us from sin's power—we are no longer enslaved to sin. However, we still struggle with sin and live in a world broken by sin.

Glorification: One day, we'll experience freedom from sin's presence when future grace leads us into glory.

Although Paul didn't pen the hymn, he understood the phrase, "Amazing grace, how sweet the sound!"[4]

25. **As you think about your adoption into the family of God (Eph. 1:5), read Romans 8:12-17.**

   ◆   **According to this passage, how does our adoption change us?**

   ◆   **What does it mean to live according to the flesh?**

   ◆   **What does it mean to live by the Spirit?**

   ◆   **What is the relationship between our adoption and suffering?**

Our adoption doesn't just secure a future inheritance; it's a present reality. The Holy Spirit lives in us, changing us day by day to increasingly look more like Jesus. While we may still struggle with sin, we're no longer enslaved to it. We're now children of God and part of our adoption is a new nature, one that has a new power to obey God. Those who live by the flesh follow their own inclinations and desires, but those who walk by the Spirit follow God's Word and ways.

Our family resemblance to Jesus also means that we experience suffering. Just as Paul found himself in prison because of his faith, we will experience hardships because of our identity in Christ. As we live by the Spirit, our lives may come in conflict with those who are living by the flesh. Daily, we'll face temptation to give into fear and live according to sinful desires. While it may seem easier to go along with the ways of the world, our transformed nature cries out to God, "Lead [me] not into temptation, but deliver [me] from evil!" (Matt. 6:13, ESV).

26. As you consider your own life, in what ways are you tempted to live according to the flesh? Is there any area you need to cry out, "Abba Father," and seek God's forgiveness?

27. Some of us may struggle to believe that we truly have forgiveness. Are there situations from your past (or present) that fill you with shame? In what areas do you struggle to believe God's grace is enough for you?

If you ever wonder if you're too far gone for grace, let me encourage you with these verses from Ephesians.

> In him we have redemption through his blood, the forgiveness of our trespasses, according to the riches of his grace, which he lavished upon us, in all wisdom and insight.

EPHESIANS 1:7-8, ESV

I love that word, *lavished*; it brings to mind the idea of abundance. I picture arms overflowing with presents or a table overflowing with good things to eat. God has storehouses of grace—He's not going to run out. This is such good news.

28. Part of God's abundant grace to us is that He doesn't leave us in our sin. As you reflect upon your walk with God, how do you see the Spirit at work in your life, transforming you to be increasingly holy and blameless?

29. Look back at verses 6, 12, and 14. What repeated word do you notice in these verses? What is Paul's ultimate hope for our lives as believers?

You were created for one purpose and one purpose only—to glorify God forever. Everything about you, from your personality to your gifts and interests (to whether you have curly or straight hair), was designed intentionally by God to reflect His glory to the world. In another of his New Testament letters, Paul wrote, "So, whether you eat or drink, or whatever you do, do all to the glory of God" (1 Cor. 10:31, ESV). And the Westminster Shorter Catechism sums it up this way: "Q: What is the chief end of man? A: Man's chief end is to glorify God and enjoy him forever."[5] You are sealed in Christ through the Spirit to praise the name of your heavenly Father forever. If you ever wonder, *Who am I and why am I here?* Ephesians 1 tells you clearly: You're a saint created by God to live to the praise of God's glory!

Paul closes his one long sentence with a reminder of the Holy Spirit's seal on your life. Typically, a seal is offered as a guarantee or confirmation. To apply for a driver's license, I'm not allowed to just use a copy of a birth certificate, I have to have one that has an embossed seal to authenticate the truthfulness of the certificate. In medieval times, a king would press his ring into wax to create an official seal for his decree before it was sent out.[6] Seals serve as a confirmation or proof that something is true.

30. What does it mean that we are sealed with the Holy Spirit?

31. According to Ephesians 1:13, what two things happened before we were sealed with the Holy Spirit?

In this opening benediction, Paul is gazing on salvation as if he's beholding a masterpiece. He's looking at it from every angle—stepping back and seeing the entire view, and at the same time zooming in and noticing every important brush stroke. He's helping us begin to comprehend the incomprehensible work of Christ on our behalf, the good news of the gospel that we first "heard" and then "believed."

Paul reminds us of the past, present, and future aspects of our salvation. He shows us the blessings of the triune God on our behalf: how the Father, Son, and Holy Spirit work in perfect unity to secure our adoption. He reminds us that our redemption has been fully purchased by Christ's blood and that forgiveness is freely granted according to the riches of His grace.

These truths are foundational for everything Paul's going to talk about in the rest of Ephesians. Paul's letter is a study of faith (what we believe) and practice (how we live out what we believe). Both faith and practice matter, but the order matters too. First, he wants us to understand what God has done on our behalf. Then, he's going to explain how we live in light of that understanding.

Reflect ───────────────

Finish your study today in prayer, asking God to allow these truths to be on your heart and mind as you go about your day. Use these words to guide you:

"Oh, the heaped up happiness of those whose God is the Lord; a happiness so great and so glorious, it cannot be conceived, and cannot be uttered! All the blessings to this world cannot make us happy, except we have you."[7]

DAY FOUR

EPHESIANS 1:15-23

Memory Verse:

Blessed is the God and Father of our Lord Jesus Christ, who has blessed us with every spiritual blessing in the heavens in Christ.

Ephesians 1:3

FROM PRAISE TO PRAYER

Read or listen to Ephesians 1 again.

What are you thankful for today? What we're thankful for tells us a lot about what we value. In the same way, what we pray for tells us a lot about what we desire. In today's study, we're moving from Paul's praise for God to his prayer for the Ephesians. Just like Ephesians 1:3-14, this section of prayer is all one sentence in the original Greek. This makes Ephesians 1 just two sentences long!

As you work through the chapter again, pay careful attention to what's on Paul's heart as he prays for the Ephesians. We'll spend today observing what the text says in Ephesians 1:15-23 before transitioning to interpretation and application tomorrow.

Now reread Ephesians 1:15-23.

32. Why does Paul give thanks for the Ephesians?

33. <u>Underline</u> the phrase *what is* in verses 18-19 (p. 13). **What three specific things does Paul pray that they would know?**

◆ What is _____

◆ What is _____

◆ What is _____

34. As you read this passage, what do you learn about:

God the Father	God the Son	God the Spirit

As Paul did in his opening praise, he again appeals to all three Persons of the Trinity in his prayer for the Ephesian saints. He prayed that they would understand not only who God is in His three Persons, but also the role each Person plays in the life of a Christ follower. Why was this concept so important to Paul? Understanding who God is and what He's done for us empowers us to live a life of godliness. Knowing God is the foundation for glorifying God.

Paul's prayer for believers includes several specific petitions that he takes to God on their behalf, which are found in verses 17-19. Let's briefly consider each one.

35. Why do you think Paul prays that God would give them the Spirit (or "a spirit") of wisdom and revelation in the knowledge of Him (v. 17)? If they already believe in Jesus, what is Paul praying for now?

36. From the context, what do you think it means to have the "eyes of your heart" enlightened (v. 18)?

When we become Christians, we know God, but we don't know everything about Him. We'll spend our entire lives "increasing in the knowledge of God" (Col. 1:10, ESV). When Paul prays for "the Spirit of wisdom and revelation," he is praying that the Spirit will be at work so that the Ephesians may know God more fully.

This desire for spiritual growth is the very reason you're doing this study right now. As you walk with God and study His Word, you can do so with anticipation. The Spirit is at work, guiding you and teaching you—opening the eyes of your heart so you might know God better!

37. **Have you ever had a time when you began to understand a spiritual truth in a new way? Or a moment when you felt like you went from being spiritually blind to being able to see spiritual truths more clearly? How does growing in the knowledge of God encourage you in your faith?**

Paul prays that they might know "what is the hope of his calling" (v. 18). Read the following verses:

> *Now may the God of hope fill you with all joy and peace as you believe so that you may overflow with hope by the power of the Holy Spirit.*
>
> **ROMANS 15:13**

> *Therefore, with your minds ready for action, be sober-minded and set your hope completely on the grace to be brought to you at the revelation of Jesus Christ. As obedient children, do not be conformed to the desires of your former ignorance. But as the one who called you is holy, you also are to be holy in all your conduct.*
>
> **1 PETER 1:13–15**

38. **From these verses, what (or whom) is the basis of our hope? What are we to set our hope on?**

39. **How does our future hope impact our present living?**

Hope is powerful. However, it's not enough to just be a hopeful person. The Object of our hope is the Source of our power. And Peter reminds us: set your hope completely on Jesus!

Paul also prays that they might know "what is the wealth of his glorious inheritance in the saints" (v. 18).

40. **Read 1 Peter 1:3-5. What do you learn about your inheritance from this passage? Why is your inheritance secure?**

As you read about the inheritance in Ephesians 1:18, you may wonder: *Is this passage talking about God's inheritance in His people or His people's inheritance, which they receive from Him?* Pastor John Stott offers this insight:

> *The Greek expression, like the English, could mean either God's inheritance or ours, that is, either the inheritance he receives or the inheritance he gives. Some commentators take it in the former sense and understand it to refer to the inheritance which God possesses among his people. Certainly the Old Testament authors taught consistently that God's people were his inheritance or 'possession' . . . But the parallel passage in Colossians 1:12 strongly suggests the other interpretation here, namely that 'God's inheritance' refers to what he will give us, for we are to give thanks to the Father, 'who has qualified you to share in the inheritance of his holy people in the kingdom of light'. In this case, if God's 'call' points back to the beginning of our Christian life, God's 'inheritance' points on to its end, to that final inheritance of which the Holy Spirit is the guarantee (14) and which Peter describes as "an inheritance that can never perish, spoil or fade kept in heaven for you.*[8]

In some sense, both concepts are true. God considers His people His inheritance; we are a treasured possession to God! And He also gives us an inheritance. It's fully secure, not dependent on our performance, but dependent upon His grace. We are beloved by God and we are blessed by God.

41. **Lastly, Paul prays that they might know "what is the immeasurable greatness of his power" (v. 19). Go back to the Ephesians text on pages 12-13 and** circle **each occurrence of the word** power **in 1:15-23.**

42. Now also read 2 Peter 1:3-4. **What do you learn about God's power from these passages? How is His power at work in the life of a believer?**

43. Read back over Ephesians 1:20-21. **List everything Paul affirms about Jesus in these two verses.**

44. **What do you learn about the relationship between Christ and the church from Ephesians 1:22-23? What does it mean that the church is His body?**

Paul closed his prayer with the culminating power of Jesus's resurrection and ascension to God's "right hand." From this place of authority Jesus governs His church, which is so closely united with Him that Paul refers to it as His "body." Don't forget this picture, it's one we'll see again and again throughout Ephesians.

Today, we've looked in depth at Paul's prayer for the Ephesians. He wasn't afraid to boldly ask for the Lord to grow their faith so that they would abound in hope. So often we feel powerless, because we forget our access to the Father's power. God's resources are available to us through prayer— any time and any place. However, sometimes I think we are hesitant to go before the Lord because we fear we aren't good enough to ask for His help.

My husband, Mike, is a seminary professor and president, and some students are intimidated to knock on his door and ask him a question. One student told me that she was so nervous that she walked back and forth and practiced what she was going to say with a friend until she had the courage to finally go in. Thankfully, she survived!

That same week I had taken my kids to Mike's office. They bounded in the room without knocking. They sat in his chair and spun around and put on his robe. They weren't intimidated in the least. Why? Because they knew that they were his beloved children. What they knew about their dad made them feel safe and secure in his presence. In the same way, what we know about God informs how we relate to Him. When you're adopted as His child, you can boldly come into His presence. He delights in you. He loves you. He welcomes you. You have the same access Paul had to God.

Reflect ——————————————————

I encourage you, take the time right now to spend some time in prayer. Use Paul's words in Ephesians 1:17-19 to guide you. You're a beloved daughter, and your Father delights to talk with you.

IT MATTERS WHO YOU KNOW

EPHESIANS 1:15-23

Memory Verse:

Blessed is the God and Father of our Lord Jesus Christ, who has blessed us with every spiritual blessing in the heavens in Christ.

Ephesians 1:3

Read through Ephesians 1 for the final time this week. By now Paul's words should be very familiar!

As we conclude our study this week, it's helpful to consider how Ephesians 1 fits into the overall structure of Paul's letter. Paul is extremely purposeful as he writes. He spends the first three chapters focusing on indicative statements (what is true about what God has done, is doing, or will do) and then moves to the imperative instructions (how we live in light of these truths). An example of how indicative and imperative statements work is something like this:

Indicative: "There's a fire in the building."

Imperative: "Get out of the building!"

Understanding the indicatives helps us understand the reasons for the imperatives. The order matters. Think of the difference between these two statements:

You are saved, therefore live a life of holiness to please the Lord.

Live a life of holiness to please the Lord so that you can be saved.

The first statement sets us free, the second one enslaves us to fear. Knowing what is true is vital for living in the truth of what we know. Therefore, Paul spends three chapters filling our minds with the good news of God's work on our behalf to secure our salvation.

Paul also knows that the only way we can understand the truth of the gospel is by the Spirit's power. For that reason, he's on his knees in prayer for the church of Ephesus. We'll close out our time in Ephesians 1 today by looking more in depth at Paul's prayer and taking the time to consider how his words can guide our prayers.

45. Now reread Ephesians 1:15-23. In what ways is Paul's prayer similar to your prayers? In what ways is it different?

46. Considering Paul's current circumstances, is there anything you're surprised Paul *didn't* pray here?

47. One thing Paul particularly prays for is that the Ephesians would know the "hope of his [God's] calling" (v. 18), which refers to God's saving grace in their lives. Take a moment to read the following verses and consider: What are some false hopes that we might be tempted to trust in instead of the hope we have in Christ?

   ◆ 1 Timothy 6:17

   ◆ Psalm 33:16-17

   ◆ Proverbs 28:26

48. In what ways are you tempted to put your hope in money, power, or your own efforts?

49. How does trusting in "false hopes" hinder our prayer lives? What keeps you from a more active prayer life?

It's so tempting to trust in what we can see to provide for what we need. We feel more at ease when we have plenty of money in our checking accounts. We feel safe because we have alarm systems. We tend to trust in our own experience or insights. It's a good thing to save our money, lock our doors, and be thoughtful in our ways! However, we need a more secure place to put our trust. Only God is able to give us the provision, security, and wisdom we need. Trusting in God gives us a secure hope for whatever circumstances we may encounter, and no matter what is going on around us, the best action we can always take is to turn to God in prayer.

50. Now read Colossians 1:9-14. How does this passage compare to Ephesians 1? Take a moment to mark similar words and phrases.

51. What do you learn about some of Paul's greatest hopes from his prayers?

52. Paul tells the Ephesians, "I never stop giving thanks for you as I remember you in my prayers." What can we learn about Paul's prayer life from this one simple statement?

53. What are a couple of specific ways you would like to grow your own prayer life, both in the frequency and the content of your prayers?

Prayer is one of the distinct features of Paul's letters. In the midst of his travels and imprisonments, he consistently prayed for the church. Prayer was a vital aspect of Paul's relationship with God and his relationship with others. He loved God, so he prayed to Him. He loved others, so he prayed for them. Paul understood that he couldn't always be with the various churches that he loved, but he could always be remembering them in his prayers.

In verse 20, Paul shifts his prayer to include a description of Christ's power. The church in Ephesus likely needed this reminder because, as one Bible commentator points out, "The message that the emperors were warrior gods, defeating their foes and bringing order to the world, appeared on coins and the reliefs of imperial altars (one of them found in Ephesus). Sometimes this imagery depicted the warrior emperor trampling his enemies underfoot."[9]

54. **In what ways do you think Paul's description of Christ's power in Ephesians 1:20-23 may have particularly encouraged the church in Ephesus? Which words or phrases stand out to you?**

It's easy to be pessimistic about the state of the world. Every day on the news we see images of violence, ungodliness, pain, and suffering. It can look like everything is spiraling out of control. The Ephesians would have experienced this sense of cultural dismay as well. However, Paul reminded them (and us): Jesus is on His throne! He reigns with power and dominion in this age and in the one to come. Everything is subject to Him. This knowledge gives us needed hope as we live our daily lives.

Paul closes his prayer by alluding to a theme that will show up throughout the book of Ephesians—unity within the church. Paul gives a first hint of this concept when he describes the church as a "body" and Christ as our "head" (vv. 22-23).

55. Read Romans 12:3-6. **What does it mean that we are part of a body? How should we think about our role in the life of the church?**

I've found Paul's explanation of the body to be such helpful imagery. Each of us is unique in our gifting. I may serve in one area and you may serve in another. Both of us are needed! When I see another believer using her gifts in a wonderful way, that doesn't mean I should do what she's doing. We've all been entrusted with spiritual gifts that we use to serve one another, to the glory of God. Our individual gifts are intended to promote unity within the church as God works in diverse ways through His people.

Both Paul's praise and Paul's prayer in Ephesians 1 highlight an overarching theme: It matters who you know. And it matters what you know about who you know. Paul's benediction serves as a reminder to the Ephesians of the spiritual blessings that belong to them in Christ. It's a terrible tragedy to be rich beyond measure and live like the poorest of paupers. Paul is desperate for them to know the hope of their calling, the riches of their inheritance, and the resurrection power that is at work in them through the Holy Spirit.

Reflect ——————————————————

Close your week of study by writing out from memory the spiritual blessings that are yours in Christ. (If you're having trouble recalling them, make it a point to memorize them before you reach the end of the next week of study. They're worth knowing by heart.)

As you write out each one, say a prayer for someone you love. Ask God to open the spiritual eyes of their heart so they may know the riches of their inheritance and set their hope fully on God's grace, not their circumstances or efforts.

Just as Paul prayed for the Ephesians, we want to live a life of praise to God and prayer for one another.

WATCH

Watch the Session Two video and take notes below.

TO ACCESS THE VIDEO SESSIONS, USE THE INSTRUCTIONS
IN THE BACK OF YOUR BIBLE STUDY BOOK.

DISCUSS

Discuss the following questions with your Bible study group. A more extensive leader guide is available for free download at **lifeway.com/ephesiansstudy**.

1. Which day of personal study had the most impact on you, and why? What lingering questions do you have?

2. How did what you heard on the video clarify, reinforce, or give new insight to what you studied this session?

3. Discuss how understanding the importance of being "in Christ" (the teddy bear and the box imagery) impacts the way you understand the spiritual blessings of Ephesians 1.

4. What is one way you can adjust your prayers for others based on Paul's example in Ephesians 1:15-19?

5. How do you want to live differently in the week to come because of what we've studied this week?

EPHESIANS 2

ALIVE & UNIFIED

In chapter 1, Paul reminded the Ephesians (and us) of God's redemptive work for His people. God blessed us, chose us, adopted us, redeemed us, and lavished His grace upon us. Before the foundation of the world, God had a plan for salvation that He set forth in Christ. In chapter 2, Paul shifts his focus from God's glory to the condition of the Ephesians before they knew Christ—they were alienated from God and from one another.

As we study chapter 2 this week, we'll consider how the graciousness of God gives us communion with God and communion with His people. We're not left dead in our sins, but we're given new life in such a way that we abound in good works that glorify God as we serve others. We change from death to life, from alienation to unification. Belonging to Christ transforms every aspect of our lives.

Melissa

EPHESIANS 2

FROM DEATH TO LIFE

[1]And you were dead in your trespasses and sins [2] in which you previously walked according to the ways of this world, according to the ruler of the power of the air, the spirit now working in the disobedient. [3] We too all previously lived among them in our fleshly desires, carrying out the inclinations of our flesh and thoughts, and we were by nature children under wrath as the others were also. [4] But God, who is rich in mercy, because of his great love that he had for us, [5] made us alive with Christ even though we were dead in trespasses. You are saved by grace! [6] He also raised us up with him and seated us with him in the heavens in Christ Jesus, [7] so that in the coming ages he might display the immeasurable riches of his grace through his kindness to us in Christ Jesus. [8] For you are saved by grace through faith, and this is not from yourselves; it is God's gift— [9] not from works, so that no one can boast. [10] For we are his workmanship, created in Christ Jesus for good works, which God prepared ahead of time for us to do.

UNITY IN CHRIST

[11] So, then, remember that at one time you were Gentiles in the flesh—called "the uncircumcised" by those called "the circumcised," which is done in the flesh by human hands. [12] At that time you were without Christ, excluded from the citizenship of Israel, and foreigners to the covenants of promise, without hope and without God in the world. [13] But now in Christ Jesus, you who were far away have been brought near by the blood of Christ. [14] For he is our peace, who made both groups one and tore down the dividing wall of hostility. In his flesh, [15] he made of no effect the law consisting of commands and expressed in regulations, so that he might create in himself one new man from the two, resulting in peace. [16] He did this so that he might reconcile both to God in one body through the cross by which he put the hostility to death. [17] He came and proclaimed the good news of peace to you who were far away and peace to those who were near. [18] For through him we both have access in one Spirit to the Father. [19] So, then, you are no longer foreigners and strangers, but fellow citizens with the saints, and members of God's household, [20] built on the foundation of the apostles and prophets, with Christ Jesus himself as the cornerstone. [21] In him the whole building, being put together, grows into a holy temple in the Lord. [22] In him you are also being built together for God's dwelling in the Spirit.

DAY ONE
1

EPHESIANS 2:1–10

Memory Verse: For you are saved by grace through faith, and this is not from yourselves; it is God's gift—not from works, so that no one can boast. For we are his workmanship, created in Christ Jesus for good works, which God prepared ahead of time for us to do.
Ephesians 2:8-10

BUT GOD

Begin by reading all of Ephesians 2.

Last week, we looked at two packed full sentences from Paul: one of praise and one of prayer. He highlighted the work of our triune God on our behalf, and he prayed that we might know the hope of our calling, the riches of our inheritance, and the resurrection power that is at work in our lives as believers. All of this is such good news. As we'll see this week, these truths only increase in grandeur as we grow in our understanding of the depths from which we've been saved.

Think of it this way: A hot shower feels good on a typical day, but if you're caked in sweat and mud and covered in filthy clothes, a hot shower is transformative. If you consider yourself somewhat okay and think that God is lucky to have you on His team, then the message of Christ's work on your behalf may seem rather ho hum. However, when you start to understand the corrosive effects of sin—how we are broken beyond human repair and unable to fix ourselves—only then can you truly begin to hope in the good news of the gospel.

This is what Paul does for us at the start of Ephesians 2. He takes a moment to remind us of *who we were* so that we'll better understand the grace of *who we're becoming*.

1. Now reread Ephesians 2:1-10. **List out everything you learn about the Ephesians before they were "saints" (vv. 1-3).**

2. **Last week you underlined "according to" regarding God's works (Eph. 1:3-14). Turn to page 46 and <u>underline</u> the two occurrences of this same phrase in verses 2:1-10, regarding how we previously lived. What were we living "according to"?**

3. Theologians often explain the three enemies of the Christian as the world (its sinful enticements and patterns), the flesh (our inward sinful desires), and the devil. How do you see these three enemies in verses 1-3?

◆ The world

◆ The flesh

◆ The devil

4. What does it mean that we were "by nature children under wrath" (v. 3)?

In chapter 1, Paul pulled back the curtain to reveal the beauty, goodness, graciousness, and loving-kindness of God. He opens chapter 2 by revealing the state of humanity apart from God's intervention. We're not just a little bit bad. We're not just a little bit broken. Without the Holy Spirit, *we're dead.*

As in, not alive. Unable to move toward God. Unable to change. Unable to get to the doctor for help. Too late for anything but a miracle of resurrection. It's not good, and it's the universal condition of every human soul. Thankfully, Paul's not finished, because he utters the two transformational words on which all of our eternity rests: But God.

5. Read verses 4-7 again. What does this passage tell us about God's character (look for descriptive words) and God's actions (look for the verbs)?

6. According to these verses, why did God save us? Take a moment to write out in your own words an explanation of why God saves someone.

But God. The best two words of sweet relief we can hear. They interrupt Paul's description of broken, sinful humanity with a stunning twist, moving our eyes off of ourselves and turning them back to God. Paul reminds us of who we were so that he can highlight the glory and wonder of God's mercy, love, and grace. God didn't save us because we were good enough, but because His love was great enough to rescue us from our sinful choices. And His love doesn't leave us in our sin; it transforms us to walk in newness of life.

7. Now read Ephesians 2:8-10. Look up the words grace and faith in a dictionary or online search and note the definitions that best fit with how they are used here.

GRACE	
FAITH	

8. From Ephesians 2:8-10, how is a person saved? What is the outworking of salvation?

9. Read Ephesians 2:4-7 once more, and circle the word *rich* or *riches*. What two things does God have an abundance of? In what ways does that encourage you today?

Our passage today reminds us of who we once were and how we lived before we were saved. Paul's words aren't meant to make us feel ashamed about our past, they are intended to show us the loving-kindness of God. Paul explains the foundation of our faith—we are saved by grace alone. Neither our good works, nor our talents, nor our engaging personality could make us alive. Only the resurrection power of God can move us from death to life.

You may think your past is worse than other people around you. You may have years and years of heartache from past mistakes and sinful choices. Or you may have a hard time imagining you were ever a child of wrath. While each of our stories may appear different in the world's eyes, we all share the same reality. We were all dead, following the ways of the world, satisfying the lusts of our flesh, and doing the works of the devil (1 John 3:8). The outward effects of our decay may look different, but the inward reality of death was true for each of us.

But God.

God loved us and He made us alive, saving us by His grace. That's our real story. That's the one that will live on through eternity, the story we'll be recounting through the ages. Once we were blind, deaf, and lame. Now we can see, hear, and walk in a manner worthy of the gospel. What we know about God changes everything we understand about ourselves. If we want to know our true identity, it starts with those two words: *But God.*

Reflect

Take some time to pray today, thanking God for the way He saved you. If you're not yet saved, or worried that you're too far gone for God to work in your life, know that these words are true for you today. Put your faith in Jesus—He loves you, He's rich in mercy and grace, and He offers you the free gift of salvation. Put your trust in Him, and you'll experience the transforming hope and sweet relief of those words, "But God."

DAY TWO
2

EPHESIANS 2:1-10

Memory Verse: For you are saved by grace through faith, and this is not from yourselves; it is God's gift—not from works, so that no one can boast. For we are his workmanship, created in Christ Jesus for good works, which God prepared ahead of time for us to do.
Ephesians 2:8-10

GOD'S MASTERPIECE

Read Ephesians 2.

After observing the text of Ephesians 2:1-10, we'll spend today further considering these verses, seeking to understand them and apply them to our own lives.

Reread Ephesians 2:1-10.

10. **Take a moment to fill out the following chart, comparing and contrasting everything you learn about your old life and your new life from this passage.**

Old Life	New Life
Ex: Dead in trespasses	Alive with Christ

Before God made us alive in Christ, we lived under the wrath of God because our sins had rightly earned His displeasure. Pastor John Stott explains,

> God's wrath is not like human anger. It is not bad temper, so that he may fly off the handle at any moment. It is neither spite, nor malice, nor hostility, nor revenge. It is never arbitrary, since it is the divine reaction to only one situation, namely evil. Therefore, it is entirely predictable, and it is never subject to mood, whim or impulse.[1]

God's wrath is nothing like what happens when someone explodes in a fit of rage or lashes out in anger. His wrath on sin is a right administration of His holiness. It is in every way a good reaction to our wrong doing. Stott continues,

> So Paul moves from the wrath of God to the mercy and love of God without any sense of embarrassment or anomaly. He is able to hold them together in his mind because he believed that they were held together in God's character. We need, I think, to be more grateful to God for his wrath, and to worship him that he always reacts to evil in the same unchanging, predictable, uncompromising way because his righteousness is perfect. Without his moral consistency we could enjoy no peace.[2]

11. **In what ways is God's judgment of evil a right and good thing? Why would it be unloving and unjust for God to ignore sin?**

12. **There is only one way for us to receive forgiveness for our sins in a manner that upholds both God's mercy and His justice. Look back at Ephesians 1:7. In what ways do we see both the love of God and the divine judgment of God at the cross?**

Our world is full of injustice. So many suffer because of the evil actions of others. Yet we can confidently proclaim, "I know that the Lord will maintain the cause of the afflicted, and will execute justice for the needy" (Ps. 140:12, ESV). Every single sin will be dealt with justly. While human courts may fail, nothing will escape the righteousness and goodness of God. This includes every sin committed against us, as well as every sin we commit.

The cross is the ultimate display of both God's divine justice and His gracious love. Christ takes the punishment for our sin. God redeems our souls, not by ignoring our sin, but by taking the punishment on our behalf, "He himself bore our sins in his body on the tree, that we might die to sin and live to righteousness. By his wounds you have been healed" (1 Pet. 2:24, ESV). At the cross, the righteousness of God and the love of God meet in a spectacular display of grace.

13. **Read the following verses, noting what you learn about the world, the flesh, and the devil.**

◆ Galatians 4:3-5 (world)

◆ Romans 8:3-9 (flesh)

◆ 1 John 3:7-8 (devil)

The world, the flesh, and the devil continue to wage war against God's people. As we'll see in Ephesians 6, there's a spiritual battle raging around us. The devil wants to steal, kill, and destroy us (John 10:10) by enticing us to follow our fleshly desires and walk in the pattern of this world. Peter reminds us, "Be sober-minded, be alert. Your adversary the devil is prowling around like a roaring lion, looking for anyone he can devour" (1 Pet. 5:8).

14. **In each of the verses above, how did God rescue us from the world, the flesh, and the devil?**

Later in Ephesians we'll consider how we take up the armor of God and do battle. For today, I want you to rest in this fact: Jesus has already won. His blood has redeemed us from slavery. Through His death and resurrection, He has destroyed the devil's works. However, the devil is still active in our world, so Jesus prayed for our protection, "I am not praying that you take them out of the world but that you protect them from the evil one" (John 17:15), and He currently intercedes on our behalf (Rom. 8:34). Yes, we have enemies, but we are not alone. We do not walk in fear of Satan's schemes—we walk by faith in God's power.

15. Compare Ephesians 2:6 with Ephesians 1:20-23. What does it mean that we are seated in the heavens in Christ Jesus? In what way is that encouraging to you as you fight against sin?

In 1:20, Paul described Jesus as seated at the right hand of God the Father "in the heavens." Now in 2:6, Paul says the same about you, me, and every person who has been saved by the blood of Jesus. No, we aren't physically there now, and our battle with sin rages on while we're in this broken world. But because of Jesus, we have assurance of our eternal place with God, and through the power of the Holy Spirit we live as kingdom citizens even today.

16. Which of these equations best describes the relationship between faith, salvation, and good works as described in Ephesians 2:8-10?

   a. Faith + Works = Salvation

   b. Faith = Salvation + Works

   c. Faith = Salvation

We're not saved by our good works; we're saved by faith in Jesus alone. But we are saved *for* good works. The beauty of God's grace is on display as our lives are changed from the inside out. God first rescues us from our old life of sin (salvation) and then increasingly transforms us to be more like Jesus (sanctification). The freedom of His grace doesn't mean we're free to sin more. It means we're free to walk in newness of life (Rom. 6:4).

17. In what ways do you attempt to earn God's favor through your works? What's the problem with that type of living? How do these verses encourage you today?

18. **What would it look like to use your gifts to serve others with humility, rightly understanding that your giftedness is the result of God's work in your life?**

I've been walking with Jesus for more than thirty-five years. When I was fifteen, I memorized Ephesians 2:8-10 in a Bible study. The words amazed me then and they still amaze me today. Grace is a gift! Salvation is free. I can't do anything to earn my adoption. God has sought me and His blood has secured me. I'm His. It's such good news. And yet, the older I get, the more impatient I can be with my need for grace. It was one thing to need grace as a new believer, but it's just embarrassing to keep needing more and more grace so many years later. Maybe I mistakenly thought by this point I'd be able to get by fine on my own. However, I find myself still having to deal with unkind thoughts, impatient sighs, angry reactions, and critical words (among many other things).

Here's the reality I've had to learn: I'll never graduate from my need of grace. On this side of eternity, I'm going to struggle with sin (see Phil. 3:12 and Matt. 6:12). However, there's still good news. God is working to change me. It may be slow going, but He's at work. And there's even better news. He has immeasurable riches of grace—He's not going to run out. His grace saves us. His grace sanctifies us. And one day, His grace will take us home.

Reflect ──────────────────────────

Take a moment to consider your own life. In what way do you feel the enticement of the world, the sinful desire of the flesh, or the attack of the evil one? As you consider these temptations today, what truths about Jesus's power encourage you?

_____

_____

_____

_____

Close your time today in prayer, praising God for both the goodness of His justice and the graciousness of His mercy. Consider injustice in the world today, and pray for God's righteousness to reign. As you think of friends and family who are dead in their sins, pray that God's mercy might awaken their hearts and make them alive in Christ. Pray that you would live faithfully as God's workmanship, created in Christ Jesus for good works.

_____

_____

_____

_____

_____

_____

_____

EPHESIANS 2:11-22

Memory Verse: For you are saved by grace through faith, and this is not from yourselves; it is God's gift—not from works, so that no one can boast. For we are his workmanship, created in Christ Jesus for good works, which God prepared ahead of time for us to do.
Ephesians 2:8-10

BUT NOW

Read through Ephesians 2 again.

Paul began chapter 2 by describing our separation from God and reconciliation to God through Christ (2:1-10). As he continues on in chapter 2, he shifts his focus to our separation from and reconciliation to one another. Paul is writing primarily to Gentiles (everyone who is not Jewish) and explains the deep separation that has existed between these two groups.

19. Read Ephesians 2:11-22. **List everything you learn about Gentiles in this passage.**

20. Now read Genesis 17:6-12. **Who was to be circumcised? When? Why?**

Circumcision represented the outward sign of God's covenant with Abraham. God promised to make Abraham into a great nation, with as many descendants as the stars in the sky or sand on the seashore (Gen. 22:17). He also promised that all the nations of the earth would be blessed by Abraham's offspring, which was ultimately fulfilled in Jesus (Gen. 22:18).

21. **What happened to change the division between Gentile and Jewish people (Eph. 2:13-15)?**

22. Read through Ephesians 2:11-22. <u>Underline</u> each occurrence of the word *peace*. **What do you learn about peace from this passage?**

The Jewish temple in Jerusalem was surrounded by a wall with an inscription, "No foreigner may enter within the barrier and enclosure round the temple. Anyone who is caught doing so will have himself to blame for his ensuing death."[3] Only descendants of Abraham were allowed within the temple and a physical wall was erected to separate Jew from Gentile. Not only were the Gentiles separated physically, but they were also separated spiritually. They didn't have the promises of Scripture, the hope of a Messiah, or knowledge of the one true God. Jews looked down on Gentiles, considering them "dogs" (Matt. 15:25-27).

However, Jesus came to save all people. Matthew's Gospel describes Jesus's encounter with a Roman centurion (a Gentile military leader). The man sought out Jesus's healing power and affirmed Jesus's authority. Jesus's response helps us understand the unifying nature of His redemptive work:

> *When Jesus heard this, He was amazed. Turning to those who were following Him, He said, "I tell you the truth, I haven't seen faith like this in all Israel! And I tell you this, that many Gentiles will come from all over the world— from east and west—and sit down with Abraham, Isaac, and Jacob at the feast in the Kingdom of Heaven."*
>
> MATTHEW 8:10-11, NLT

Jesus's ministry of reconciliation unites us in God's eternal kingdom. The dividing wall of hostility is broken down! Jesus is the ultimate fulfillment of God's promise to Abraham, "all the nations of the earth will be blessed by your offspring" (Gen. 22:18).

23. **Paul tells them they are no longer "foreigners and strangers" but "citizens and household members" (Eph. 2:19). What's the difference between being a foreigner and a citizen? What about between being a stranger and a household member?**

If you've ever traveled outside of your home country, you know the feeling of being a foreigner. Foreigners don't have the same customs, languages, or rights as citizens. It's easy to feel lost and different from everyone else. In the same way, strangers may be welcomed into a home, but they don't have the same sense of belonging as someone who actually lives in the home. Being citizens and household members means that we belong to God in a familial way. We are welcomed into God's kingdom as beloved children coming home, not guests who are just passing through.

24. **Look up a definition for cornerstone and write it below. Based on what you find, what do you think Paul meant when he referred to Christ as "the cornerstone" (vv. 20-22)?**

CORNERSTONE

In verses 20-22, Paul used building imagery to describe the church, the unified body of Christ. The cornerstone,

> "Is itself part of and essential to the foundation; it helps to hold the building steady, and it also sets it and keeps it in line . . . Paul has particularly in mind the function of Jesus Christ in holding the growing temple together as a unity. For he is the chief cornerstone, in whom the whole structure is joined together and grows . . . As a building depends for both its cohesion and its development on being tied securely to its cornerstone, so Christ the cornerstone is indispensable to the church's unity and growth. Unless it is constantly and securely related to Christ, the church's unity will disintegrate and its growth either stop or run wild."[4]

25. **Now read back through all of Ephesians 2 one more time, looking for mentions of the Trinity. As you read, fill in the chart below, noting what you learn about the Father, Son, and Holy Spirit.**

God the Father	God the Son	God the Spirit

26. **In what way does our union with Christ unite us to one another? What imagery does Paul use to describe this unity in Ephesians 2?**

Our alienation from God resulted in alienation from one another and hostility toward one another. Thankfully, Paul offers us a hopeful solution to our problem. Remember how Paul interrupted his reflection on our separation from God with his powerful "But God" statement? He does that again in today's passage with the equally as powerful, "But now in Christ Jesus."

Our union with Christ unifies us with one another. The dividing wall of hostility is torn down. Just as Jews and Gentiles are united in Christ, as believers we are united with people from every tongue, tribe, and nation. Peace with God allows us to experience peace with one another.

The Christian faith isn't a solitary "God and me" sort of relationship. All throughout this letter, Paul speaks in plural terms—"us," "we," and "our"— terms that reflect God's relational design for His church. *But now in Christ Jesus* we belong to God and one another.

Reflect ————————————————————————

Spend some time in prayer, specifically praying for peace and unity in your relationships with other believers in the church.

DAY FOUR 4

EPHESIANS 2:11-22

Memory Verse: For you are saved by grace through faith, and this is not from yourselves; it is God's gift—not from works, so that no one can boast. For we are his workmanship, created in Christ Jesus for good works, which God prepared ahead of time for us to do. *Ephesians 2:8-10*

CIRCUMCISED HEARTS

Read Ephesians 2 from another translation if you have one available.

Now that we've observed the text of Ephesians 2:11-22, we'll look at this passage more in depth, seeking to interpret it correctly and apply it to our own lives.

Reread Ephesians 2:11-22.

Paul calls his Jewish brothers "those *called* 'the circumcised'" (2:11, emphasis mine) rather than simply "the circumcised." Consider what the following verses teach about circumcision and answer the questions that follow.

- ◆ Deuteronomy 30:6
- ◆ Jeremiah 9:25-26
- ◆ Colossians 2:11-12
- ◆ Galatians 5:6

27. **What does it mean to be circumcised in the heart?**

28. **What does it mean to be "circumcised yet uncircumcised"?**

29. **What is our new circumcision in Christ?**

The Israelites may have considered themselves better than others because of physical circumcision (Gen. 17), but Paul understood they needed circumcised hearts. They had an outer veneer of spirituality, without true heart change. I wonder if the last words of the first martyr, Stephen, continued to ring in Paul's ears, "You stiff-necked people with *uncircumcised hearts* and ears! You are always resisting the Holy Spirit" (Acts 7:51, emphasis mine).

Paul knew what it was to be circumcised in the flesh with an uncircumcised heart. He listened to Stephen's words, watched as Stephen was stoned for his testimony about Jesus, and even approved of his death (Acts 8:1). Paul continued to persecute Christians until God intervened in a miraculous blinding light experience on the road to Damascus. Paul knew firsthand that external religiosity without heart change only leads to spiritual pride and relational discord.

True circumcision isn't one of the flesh, it's a heart changed by Jesus. Abraham's descendants had an outward sign, but they still needed an inward heart transformation. We all do. This is what the prophet Jeremiah alluded to when he wrote, "I will put my teaching within them and write it on their hearts. I will be their God, and they will be my people" (Jer. 31:33).

30. **How does pride in our good works, ancestry, denomination, or even our theological understanding cause division in the church today?**

31. **What does it mean that Jesus "made of no effect the law" (v. 15)? Read the following verses for further insight into what Paul means: Matthew 5:17-20; Galatians 2:15-16; Romans 3:31.**

32. **If the law is of no effect, does it matter whether or not we obey it? Why or why not?**

Jesus came to fulfill the law on our behalf. His death paid for our sin, and His perfect life was credited to our account as righteousness. (Side note: Abraham, the spiritual father of the Jews, was also saved by this credited righteousness. See Rom. 4:9-12.) In Christ, the law has no power to condemn us any longer—it's been completely fulfilled on our behalf!

At the same time, as followers of Christ, the Spirit directs us to love God's law because we have new spiritual eyes to see its goodness (see Ps. 119). The moral law can't save us, but it does shows us what life by the Spirit looks like—it's the path of following Jesus. By grace, we walk in faith, seeking to honor God in all our ways. We do so not because the law can save us, but because God's Word guides us. As Jesus taught His followers, "Everyone then who hears these words of mine and does them will be like a wise man who built his house on the rock" (Matt. 7:24, ESV). God's Word is His grace to us—it shows us how to live wisely!

33. **Paul has used two images to describe God's people: a body and a building. How do each of those images help your understanding of what it means to be part of the church?**

◆ **Body**

◆ **Building**

Both a body and a building are full of many parts. The body has fingers and toes, eyes and ears. A building has bricks and mortar, nails and screws. Each unique part matters. Yet, on their own they wouldn't amount to much. Working together, though, they form a beautiful union where each part supports and nourishes the other.

34. **How can you live at peace with other Christians in your life? Is there any group of Christians that you find it difficult to be at peace with?**

35. **What would it look like to consider the people in your church as members of your family? How might the depth and quality of your relationships change?**

36. **What does it mean that we are a "holy temple in the Lord"? How should that impact the way we live our lives?**

By His blood, Jesus Christ gained access for us to the Father and peace with one another. He made the law of "no effect"—meaning that it no longer has the power to condemn us. We're no longer strangers to God, but beloved children. The church is the holy temple of God, the place where God meets with His people and shines His glory out into the world. We belong to the people of God and can rejoice with the psalmist, "For a day in your courts is better than a thousand elsewhere. I would rather be a doorkeeper in the house of my God than dwell in the tents of wickedness" (Ps. 84:10, ESV).

Reflect

Spend some time in prayer, thanking Jesus for perfectly fulfilling the law so that we might be reconciled to God and to one another.

DAY FIVE
5

EPHESIANS 1–2

Memory Verse: For you are saved by grace through faith, and this is not from yourselves; it is God's gift—not from works, so that no one can boast. For we are his workmanship, created in Christ Jesus for good works, which God prepared ahead of time for us to do.
Ephesians 2:8-10

IN CHRIST

We've spent the past nine lessons zooming in verse by verse as we've read through Ephesians 1 and 2. Today, I want us to zoom back out and read these two chapters all over again. Open your Bible to Ephesians and read the first two chapters with fresh eyes, as though you're opening a letter from a good friend.

37. **Did you notice anything new as you read these two chapters again? What stands out about the structure, flow, and repeated words or phrases?**

38. **The phrase translated "in the heavens" or "in the heavenly places" is a Greek phrase that is only used in the book of Ephesians, but Paul uses it five times in this letter. Look at each of the following verses and note what you learn about "in the heavens."**

1:3	
1:20	
2:6	
3:10	
6:12	

39. **Look over Ephesians 1 and 2, and <u>underline</u> each time you see the phrase, "in Christ," "in him," "in the Beloved," "in his flesh," or any other reference to being in Christ.**

In the first two chapters of Ephesians 1 and 2, we learn the most crucial part of our identity as believers—we're safely "in Christ."

- *In Christ we're blessed with every spiritual blessing.*
- *In Christ we're chosen before the foundation of the world to be holy and blameless.*
- *In Christ we have redemption.*
- *In Christ we've received an inheritance.*
- *In Christ we bring praise to His glory.*
- *In Christ we're sealed with the Holy Spirit.*
- *In Christ we're seated in the heavens.*
- *In Christ we experience the riches of His grace and kindness.*
- *In Christ we're God's masterpiece, created to do good works.*
- *In Christ we've been brought near to God.*
- *In Christ we have peace with God and peace with others.*
- *In Christ we belong together, growing as a temple to the Lord.*
- *In Christ we're being built together as a dwelling for the Spirit.*

We are who we are in Christ because of God's work in our salvation, which Paul clearly and beautifully describes in these two chapters. God:

- *Chose us before the foundation of the world (1:4)*
- *Predestined us for adoption (1:5)*
- *Made known to us the mystery of His will (1:9)*
- *Worked everything in agreement with the purpose of His will (1:11)*
- *Made us alive with Christ even though we were dead in trespasses (2:5)*
- *Saved us by grace through faith (2:8)*
- *Prepared our good works in advance for us to do (2:10).*

From start to finish our salvation is the work of God on our behalf. That means we can rest secure because our salvation isn't up to us. That doesn't mean that we are inactive participants in salvation. Ephesians 1:13 tells us that we were sealed with the Holy Spirit when we "heard the word of truth, the gospel of your salvation, and when you believed." God makes us alive in Christ when we hear the message and believe.

This is such good news, but it can be confusing as well. If God chooses some, why does He not choose others? If God is sovereign in salvation, does it matter that I share my faith with others? How do we understand the relationship between God's sovereignty and personal responsibility? Years ago in college, I read one of the most helpful books for me on this topic, *Evangelism and the Sovereignty of God* by J. I. Packer. This morning, I flipped through the well-worn pages, pondering the wisdom of Packer's words. As he discussed the truth of God's sovereignty alongside the truth of man's responsibility, he offered the following insight:

> C. H. Spurgeon was once asked if he could reconcile these two truths to each other. "I wouldn't try," he replied; "I never reconcile friends." Friends? — Yes, friends. This is the point that we have to grasp. In the Bible, divine sovereignty and human responsibility are not enemies. They are not uneasy neighbors; they are not in an endless state of cold war with each other. They are friends, and they work together.[5]

We're always limited in our comprehension of the ways God is at work in our world. We're finite creatures attempting to understand an infinite God. Our inability to comprehend God's ways shouldn't surprise us. However, we can be encouraged by two key truths: From beginning to end, God secures our salvation. *And* it's of vital importance that we share the good news of salvation in Christ with others.

In his letter to the Romans, Paul questioned, "How, then, can they call on him they have not believed in? And how can they believe without hearing about him? And how can they hear without a preacher?" (Rom. 10:14). As we go out into all the world sharing the good news of the gospel, God uses our words to save others by the power of the Holy Spirit. If we don't go, they won't hear. If God's Spirit doesn't make them alive, they can't believe. Both are true at the same time.

40. How does God's work in salvation give you comfort and thankfulness as you reflect on it today?

41. The Holy Spirit—not your persuasive or perfect words—opens people's spiritual eyes. How does this truth transform the way you think about evangelism? How does it reframe any fears or hesitations you have about sharing the gospel with others?

42. Who in your life needs to know Jesus? Personalize the words of Paul today as you pray specifically:

I pray that the eyes of _____'s

heart may be enlightened so that _____

may know what is the hope of God's calling, what is the

wealth of his glorious inheritance in the saints, and what

is the immeasurable greatness of his power toward us who

believe, according to the mighty working of his strength.

As we come to the end of our study for this week, I want to wrap up with a time of reflection considering what we've learned so far. These first two chapters in Ephesians provide us with some of the most profound truths about who God is and who we are in Christ.

43. Consider the glimpses of the Trinity Paul has provided in these first two chapters of Ephesians. Review the charts you've filled out (pp. 23, 31, and 60). Summarize what you've learned about each Person of the Trinity from Ephesians 1 and 2.

God the Father	God the Son	God the Spirit

44. While you reflect on Ephesians 1–2, write down in your own words what you've learned about your:

◆ Life Before Christ

◆ Salvation

◆ Spiritual Blessings

◆ Good Works

◆ **Union with God's people**

◆ **Hope**

◆ **Inheritance**

45. **With these spiritual blessings in mind, what are you particularly thankful for today?**

All that matters for life today and hope for tomorrow is found in Christ. We're secure because our names are written in heaven (Luke 10:20). Jesus is the reason we can always rejoice.

Reflect————————————————————————

Spend some time today in prayer, thanking God for all that is yours in Christ Jesus.

For you are saved by grace through faith, and this is not from yourselves; it is God's gift—not from works, so that no one can boast. For we are his workmanship, created in Christ Jesus for good works, which God prepared ahead of time for us to do.

EPHESIANS 2:8-10

WATCH

Watch the Session Three video and take notes below.

TO ACCESS THE VIDEO SESSIONS, USE THE INSTRUCTIONS
IN THE BACK OF YOUR BIBLE STUDY BOOK.

DISCUSS

Discuss the following questions with your Bible study group. A more extensive leader guide is available for free download at **lifeway.com/ephesiansstudy.**

1   Which day of personal study had the most impact on you, and why? What lingering questions do you have?

2   How did what you heard on the video clarify, reinforce, or give new insight to what you studied this session?

3   In today's video, the authors shared their experiences of moving from spiritual death to life in Christ (Eph. 2:1-10). Take some time now to share your own stories.

4   What stood out to you from the conversation around the body and building imagery in Ephesians 2:11-22? What are the implications for your local church involvement?

5   How do you want to live differently in the week to come because of what we've studied this week?

EPHESIANS 3

MYSTERY & POWER

This week, we're beginning our transition from Paul's focus on orthodoxy—telling us what to believe about God—to Paul's focus on orthopraxy—telling us how that belief should impact our behavior. We'll get the first hints of our marching orders for living out our faith, but we're not stepping out of that listening and receiving mode just yet.

In chapter 3, Paul reveals a beautiful mystery to us, one that changed the first-century church's understanding of who makes up the body of Christ. We'll take what we've learned about God's plan and His character and watch how that love expands the family of faith.

Jasmine

EPHESIANS 3

PAUL'S MINISTRY TO THE GENTILES

For this reason, I, Paul, the prisoner of Christ Jesus on behalf of you Gentiles— ² assuming you have heard about the administration of God's grace that he gave me for you. ³ The mystery was made known to me by revelation, as I have briefly written above. ⁴ By reading this you are able to understand my insight into the mystery of Christ. ⁵ This was not made known to people in other generations as it is now revealed to his holy apostles and prophets by the Spirit: ⁶ The Gentiles are coheirs, members of the same body, and partners in the promise in Christ Jesus through the gospel. ⁷ I was made a servant of this gospel by the gift of God's grace that was given to me by the working of his power.

⁸ This grace was given to me—the least of all the saints—to proclaim to the Gentiles the incalculable riches of Christ, ⁹ and to shed light for all about the administration of the mystery hidden for ages in God who created all things. ¹⁰ This is so that God's multi-faceted wisdom may now be made known through the church to the rulers and authorities in the heavens. ¹¹ This is according to his eternal purpose accomplished

in Christ Jesus our Lord. [12] In him we have boldness and confident access through faith in him. [13] So, then, I ask you not to be discouraged over my afflictions on your behalf, for they are your glory.

PRAYER FOR SPIRITUAL POWER

[14] For this reason I kneel before the Father [15] from whom every family in heaven and on earth is named. [16] I pray that he may grant you, according to the riches of his glory, to be strengthened with power in your inner being through his Spirit, [17] and that Christ may dwell in your hearts through faith. I pray that you, being rooted and firmly established in love, [18] may be able to comprehend with all the saints what is the length and width, height and depth of God's love, [19] and to know Christ's love that surpasses knowledge, so that you may be filled with all the fullness of God.

[20] Now to him who is able to do above and beyond all that we ask or think according to the power that works in us— [21] to him be glory in the church and in Christ Jesus to all generations, forever and ever. Amen.

EPHESIANS 3

Memory Verse: Now to him who is able to do above and beyond all that we ask or think according to the power that works in us—to him be glory in the church and in Christ Jesus to all generations, forever and ever. Amen.

Ephesians 3:20-21

THE RICHES OF CHRIST

Read Ephesians 1–3 in full.

Ephesians is helpfully divided into two distinct sections: Chapters 1–3 focus on *orthodoxy* and chapters 4–6 focus on *orthopraxy*. Put another way, chapters 1, 2, and 3 concern themselves with *right belief* and chapters 4, 5, and 6 concern themselves with *right practice*. This is not to say that orthodoxy and orthopraxy never meet in Ephesians. We find implications for our belief *and* our behavior in chapters 1–3, just as we find implications for our behavior *and* our belief in chapters 4–6. But this delineation is helpful in discerning Paul's structure and intent.

Imagine *orthodoxy* like the roots of a tree: a complex network of belief that spirals out in numerous directions, anchoring the tree to the soil, pulling up nutrients from the ground, and keeping the tree strong and upright. If enough of the root system is destroyed, the tree will ultimately die, no matter how strong its structure looks from above-ground. Imagine *orthopraxy* as the fruit that grows from the tree: the result of a mature, well-established tree with a strong, healthy root system.

1. Read the following two passages. <u>Underline</u> the word *tree;* circle the word *fruit;* put boxes around the words *good* and *evil.*

    For no good tree bears bad fruit, nor again does a bad tree bear good fruit, for each tree is known by its own fruit. For figs are not gathered from thornbushes, nor are grapes picked from a bramble bush. The good person out of the good treasure of his heart produces good, and the evil person out of his evil treasure produces evil, for out of the abundance of the heart his mouth speaks.

    LUKE 6:43-45, ESV

Either make the tree good and its fruit good, or make the tree
bad and its fruit bad, for the tree is known by its fruit. You
brood of vipers! How can you speak good, when you are evil?
For out of the abundance of the heart the mouth speaks. The
good person out of his good treasure brings forth good, and
the evil person out of his evil treasure brings forth evil. I
tell you, on the day of judgment people will give account for
every careless word they speak, for by your words you will
be justified, and by your words you will be condemned.

MATTHEW 12:33-37, ESV

2. Jesus is the speaker in both of these quotes from Luke 6 and
   Matthew 12. Where does Jesus tell us that good fruit comes from?
   Where do we find evidence of that good fruit?

3. Reflect on the phrase "abundance of the heart." What does it mean in
   this context? Where can we find this abundance Jesus speaks of?

Jesus's imagery calls to mind the possibility of arms heavy-laden with
good fruit, like a cornucopia bursting with a healthy, bountiful harvest.
That possibility does not emerge from an unhealthy root system or a
malnourished heart. In Ephesians 1–2, Paul has told us exactly where that
nourishment comes from.

4. Where do you see the language of abundance in Ephesians 1 and 2? Go
   back through chapters 1 and 2 (pp. 12-13, 46-47) and circle the word
   riches or *wealth* whenever you see it.

5. List here each time Paul uses the words *riches* and/or *wealth* to describe
   the gifts we've been given in Christ.

6. **Why is belief in these riches an important element of growth in Christ?**

At one point during His earthly ministry, Jesus described the abundant life that is possible for all who believe in Him. He said, "I have come so that they may have life and have it in abundance" (John 10:10). This is the life Paul goes to great lengths to describe in his letter to the Ephesians. Each of the mentions of riches or wealth in Ephesians 1–2 highlight the overflowing grace and glory of God in our lives because of the work of Christ Jesus on our behalf. He doesn't just give us life. He gives us abundant life that flows out of His abundant love.

7. **Now, read chapter 3 again, in full. Circle the two places that you see the word _riches_ (pp. 78-79). What are those "riches"?**

How do they relate to abundance?

Chapter 3 moves us toward the orthopraxy portion of Ephesians, but not before teaching us something else we must believe about the spiritual blessings God has extended: These riches are for the Gentiles. They are no longer just for the children of Abraham.

God's Genesis 12 promise has come full circle.

> _Now the Lord said to Abram, "Go from your country and your kindred and your father's house to the land that I will show you. And I will make of you a great nation, and I will bless you and make your name great, so that you will be a blessing. I will bless those who bless you, and him who dishonors you I will curse, and in you all the families of the earth shall be blessed."_
>
> **GENESIS 12:1-3 , ESV**

8. What does God say about the nations in His promise to Abraham?

All of the families of the earth shall be blessed. Paul has been building a case for the family of faith from the very first chapter of this book. He has laid the groundwork for our unity in Christ and for the sacrifice that purchased that unity and its eternal assurance. He brings chapter 2 to a close with the reminder that both "the circumcised" and "the uncircumcised" are members of God's single household.

In chapter 3, Paul builds upon that groundwork to tell his listeners that the spiritual blessings he's described are now available to the Gentiles too; we are all now part of the family of faith if we profess allegiance to Christ. The abundant life found in Jesus is for Jews and Gentiles alike.

Part of our healthy root system includes being rooted and grounded in unity with our brothers and sisters in Christ. We're not just lone trees in a forest of other loners, but an entire network who is one in Christ.

9. What are some things that Paul has asked you to believe in these first three chapters of Ephesians? The list need not be exhaustive, but try to think of more than three things.

10. What is at stake if you don't believe these things?

11. Who stands ready to help you with your unbelief?

Reflect

Take a few moments to pray. Focus this time on voicing your gratitude to God for the riches of His glory that are yours in Christ. Sit in silence and let the awe of God's love for you overwhelm you. If you'd like, set a timer for five minutes and see how many of the "riches of His glory" that you can write down. How has He shown these riches in your life?

GENTILE INCLUSION
IN THE GOSPEL

Paul bridges Ephesians 2 and 3 with the concept of Gentile inclusion in the gospel. In chapter 2, he described Gentiles as "you who were far away" (v. 17) but are now "fellow citizens with the saints, and members of God's household" (v. 19). Then at the start of chapter 3, Paul described himself as "the prisoner of Christ Jesus on behalf of you Gentiles" (v. 1). So why the emphasis on Gentile ministry from this first-century Jewish missionary?

Broadly defined, the term Gentiles refers to "People who are not part of God's chosen family at birth and thus can be considered 'pagans.'" [1]

After the fall and the early years of humanity's sinful existence on earth, God set apart a man—Abraham—to be the father of a nation that would be God's chosen people. God told Abraham, "I will make you into a great nation . . . and all the peoples on earth will be blessed through you" (Gen. 12:2-3). The nation of Israel was the nation set apart by God to be His people, but they were also always supposed to be His light to the world (Isa. 49:6).

Throughout Jesus's earthly ministry, He made it clear through His words and His actions that He came to bring reconciliation between God and both Jews and Gentiles. In the Great Commission, His closing instructions to His disciples, Jesus said, "Go, therefore, and make disciples of all nations" (Matt. 28:19). Paul understood this mission and the truth that at the heart of the gospel is the good news that Jesus's death and resurrection secures salvation for all people. But this was still hard for many Jewish Christians to understand.

The book of Acts and several of Paul's letters describe the progression and tension of Gentile conversion.

"At the house of Cornelius, the Spirit was poured out on the Gentiles (Acts 10:45; 11:1, 18; 15:7). The apostolic gathering in Jerusalem, by the apostolic letter, freed Gentiles from obedience to the law (Acts 15:19; compare 21:19, 21, 25).

"In the apostolic preaching the promise to Abraham (Gen. 12:3; 18:18) found fulfillment (Gal. 3:8). Though in times past the Gentiles had been without God (Eph. 2:12–22), God in Christ broke through all boundaries. Paul, sent to preach among the Gentiles (Acts 9:15; 22:21; 26:17; Gal. 1:16; 2:9) was in perils (2 Cor. 11:26). When rejected in the synagogues, he turned to the Gentiles (Acts 13:46; 18:6; 28:28), understanding his work in the light of Old Testament predictions (Acts 13:47, 48; Rom. 15:9–12). As the apostle to the Gentiles (Gal. 2:8-9), claiming that in Christ racial distinctions were obliterated (Gal. 3:28), Paul proclaimed an equal opportunity of salvation (Rom. 1:16; 9:24; Col. 3:11; compare Acts 26:20, 23). Gentiles were the wild branches in the allegory grafted into the olive tree (Rom. 11:16–25). . . .

"Paul experienced great resentment among the Jews because of the opportunity he was offering the Gentiles (Rom. 2:15–16). Nevertheless, in New Testament thought, the church made up of Jew and Gentile was the holy nation, God's own people (1 Pet. 2:9)." [2]

DAY TWO
2

EPHESIANS 3:1-7

Memory Verse: Now to him who is able to do above and beyond all that we ask or think according to the power that works in us—to him be glory in the church and in Christ Jesus to all generations, forever and ever. Amen.
Ephesians 3:20-21

TO THE GENTILES

Begin by reading through Ephesians 3 again.

Ephesians 3 is the last chapter in the first half of Paul's letter. Remember, we have been focusing on orthodoxy in Ephesians 1–2: right belief. Ephesians 4 will transition us into orthopraxy: right practice. This is not to say there won't be any overlap. The fruit of our actions comes from the abundance of what we believe about Jesus, after all. But this delineation helps us organize the book of Ephesians and wrap our minds around Paul's teaching.

Today we'll look more closely at the beginning of Ephesians 3. Ephesians 3:1-13 is made up of three distinct sections:

3:1	Paul, the prisoner on behalf of the Gentiles (3:1)
3:2-7	Paul, the steward of grace and the servant of the gospel (3:2-7)
3:8-13	The purpose and significance of Paul's gospel message (3:8-13)

12. **Read Ephesians 3:1-13 with these three sections in mind. Does anything stand out to you about these three sections?**

13. **Write Ephesians 3:1 below. Mark the words Paul uses to describe himself.**

14. Paul was in Roman captivity. Why did he describe himself as a prisoner of Christ and not the Romans? What did Paul mean when he stated that he was in prison on behalf of the Gentiles?

15. Now read 1 Thessalonians 2:14-16. What suffering and persecution does Paul relate his persecution to? What is the hindrance being placed in Paul's way?

Ephesians 2 wrapped up with Paul's emphasis on the unity of the body of Christ built on the foundation of the apostles and prophets with Christ as the cornerstone. "For this reason" (3:1) connects everything that follows in chapter 3 with that declaration of unity. The universal church is made up of individual believers, Jew and Gentile, who are filled with the Holy Spirit and united in Christ (2:21-22). Lest we take this revelation lightly, Paul pauses mid-thought to draw the readers' attention to what he has suffered in proclaiming this truth.

Read Ephesians 3:1-7 again.

Paul speaks of a mystery, but it's not a mystery in the whodunit sense that we might be used to hearing. Verse 3 tells us that this mystery has already been solved by divine revelation.

16. Bearing in mind what you've read in Ephesians 1:1–3:7, what is the "mystery" that was revealed to Paul? (Hint: focus in on 3:6.)

This isn't the only time Paul mentions a mystery—something God has revealed or illuminated for him. He uses the Greek word *mysterion* twenty-one times in his letters, six of which are in Ephesians. The mysteries he speaks of don't always concern the Gentiles, but it does concern them in two instances—Ephesians 3:1-7 and Colossians 1:24-29.

17. **Read Colossians 1:24-29. How is this passage similar to Ephesians 3:1-7? What is the gift Paul speaks of concerning the Gentiles?**

Paul realizes that this mystery was not explicitly made known to preceding generations, but that now the apostles and prophets know the truth by the Spirit: "Gentiles are fellow heirs, members of the same body, and partakers of the promise in Christ Jesus through the gospel" (Eph. 3:6, ESV). In other words, the gospel is for all people.

Now, there have been hints at this mystery all along. The Old Testament includes many stories where Gentiles take part in the promises of God. Of the five women mentioned in Jesus's genealogy, three were Gentiles: Tamar the Canaanite, Rahab of Jericho, and Ruth the Moabite (Matt.1:1-17). Another, Bathsheba, was likely an Israelite who married a Gentile—Uriah the Hittite.

18. **Why is it significant that Jesus's genealogy includes Gentiles, and more specifically Gentile women?**

Way back at the beginning of Scripture, in Genesis 3:15, God makes a pivotal promise to the first humans after they sinned. This promise, called the *protoevangelium* ("the first gospel"), is the promise to which all of Scripture points. It states, "I will put enmity between you and the woman, and between your offspring and her offspring; he shall bruise your head, and you shall bruise his heel" (ESV).

The "offspring," or the "seed of the woman," draws particular focus in this verse. It's a focus that is echoed in Matthew 1 through the inclusion of five women into a genealogy that could've just mentioned the men—at least, until it got to Mary. For the Israelites, part of the purpose of genealogies was to show ethnic purity. One might think a more affective genealogical strategy for Matthew would have been to stick to the Israelite men who comprise

Jesus's family tree. But Matthew—under the divine inspiration of the Holy Spirit—deviates, highlighting both women and Gentiles, as well as the fact that the Venn Diagram between those two categories is almost a circle when it comes to Jesus's birth.

These Gentile women offer a beautiful picture of the mystery that Paul has in view: Gentiles are coheirs, equals with the descendants of Abraham, to the promise of Christ. The time for the trickle of Gentile blood into the line of Christ has ceased—a rushing river is coming.

19. **Read Ephesians 3:7 one last time. By whose authority is Paul revealing this mystery? By whose authority is this mystery revealed as true? For whose glory have Gentiles been included into this promise?**

20. **What is the good news for you in these verses?**

Paul's words in Ephesians 3:1-7 were good news for the Gentiles in his day, and they are good news for you and me today. Because of Paul's faithfulness to minister "on behalf of you Gentiles," the gospel message made its way across continents and centuries and into your hands. Paul fought for this mystery to be made known to the Gentiles of his day, and your faith is evidence that God used him in ways he never could have imagined.

Reflect ————————————————————————

As you wrap up your study time today, reflect on how the gospel made it to you. Who did God use to make His grace known to you? Who might He be trying to influence through you? Don't take lightly the role you've been given to advance the gospel on behalf of others.

DAY THREE
3

EPHESIANS 3:8-13

Memory Verse: Now to him who is able to do above and beyond all that we ask or think according to the power that works in us—to him be glory in the church and in Christ Jesus to all generations, forever and ever. Amen.

Ephesians 3:20-21

AT WORK FOR CHRIST

Read Ephesians 3 once in full. Then reread Ephesians 3:8-13.

As we move through Ephesians 3, Paul reminds us once again of who he is:

> *This grace was given to me—*
> *the least of all the saints.*

EPHESIANS 3:8A

This is not the only time that Paul describes himself as "the least." This does not come from a false sense of modesty on Paul's part, but from a very real understanding of who he was before he was called by Christ.

You'll recall from last week that prior to meeting Jesus, Paul was a persecutor of Christians and a devout Jew with an impressive Jewish pedigree (Acts 8:1-3; 1 Cor. 15:3-11). In Philippians 3, Paul reminds his listeners of that pedigree.

> *If anyone else thinks he has grounds for*
> *confidence in the flesh, I have more: circumcised*
> *the eighth day; of the nation of Israel, of the*
> *tribe of Benjamin, a Hebrew born of Hebrews;*
> *regarding the law, a Pharisee; regarding*
> *zeal, persecuting the church; regarding the*
> *righteousness that is in the law, blameless.*

PHILIPPIANS 3:4-6

Paul was so zealous that he led persecutions against the early church with zeal, dragging early Christians out of their homes and imprisoning them. When Paul has his dramatic "road to Damascus" moment (Acts 9) the change in his life is stark.

21. **Look up the texts below to help you fill in the following chart of Paul's changes.**

Paul goes from:	To:
Relying on his circumcision	Galatians 5:2-6
Putting his faith into his ability to keep the law	Ephesians 2:8-10
Putting his stock into being of the tribe of Benjamin	Ephesians 3:1-7
Persecuting the church	Ephesians 3:8
Seeing himself as blameless under the law	1 Timothy 1:12-17

The man who persecuted Jewish Christians for their worship of Jesus and their belief that He is God is now being persecuted for bringing the gospel to the Gentiles. How can this be?

22. **Read Ephesians 3:8-10 again. For what purpose does Paul say God saved him?**

23. **Where do you see abundance language again in this passage? Mark it in your copy of the text.**

24. Remember: what is the mystery to which Paul is referring?

25. What mission does Paul say that the church has?

Paul draws his readers' attention from his suffering to God's purpose in that suffering: to bring to light for everyone the plan and mystery hidden for the ages in God. What is that plan? To make known the manifold wisdom of God everywhere. This is the mission we continue to live out as part of the global church today.

Verse 10 includes a statement of the church's mission, but it also has one of those phrases that can create a hangup for us as we try our best to interpret God's Word. Who are these rulers and authorities in heavenly places? Biblical scholar Klyne Snodgrass offers four possible interpretations:

1. *The church makes known God's wisdom to good angels (see 1 Pet. 1:12).*

2. *The church makes known God's wisdom to evil powers in order to bring about their conversion, to announce their defeat, or to cause them to marvel.*

3. *The church makes known God's wisdom to human institutions and structures to transform their actions.*

4. *Some combination of the above.*[3]

We can't know for certain what Paul had in view here, but whatever the interpretation, Paul shows us that our calling is clear: to proclaim the manifold, or multifaceted, wisdom of God.

26. Which interpretation makes the most sense to you, given the context? Does the interpretation change our mission?

27. Now read Ephesians 3:11-12. What eternal purpose has been realized in Christ Jesus?

28. What does it mean that we have boldness and access to God?

29. What can confidence in this access look like? What does it need to look like for you today?

Paul went from persecuting the church to suffering persecution on behalf of the church. He went from being struck blind by the glory of Christ to being wholly, completely forgiven and confidently asserting his sonship. This is powerful news for Paul and for us. The certainty of our faith in Christ has a profound impact on our days and our future. In Christ, our sins are forgiven (1 John 1:9). In Christ, we can pray with confidence knowing He hears our prayers and intercedes on our behalf (Rom. 8:34). In Christ, we know we are filled with the power of the Holy Spirit (Acts 1:8) to live as faithful citizens, as salt and light (Matt. 5:13-16), today. And in Christ, we know our eternal hope is secure (Rom. 8:37-39).

Read Ephesians 3:13 as we wrap up today's study.

So I ask you not to lose heart over what I am
suffering for you, which is your glory (ESV).

30. Reminder: Why is Paul suffering in prison right now?

31. Why does he say the suffering is "for you," his Gentile readers?

Paul continues to emphasize what it has cost him to bring the gospel to the Gentiles, not for his own personal glory (remember, he continues to say he is the least of these), but as a reminder to the Gentiles that someone is willing to suffer so that they may hear and know the gospel. Snodgrass again:

> The thought that Paul's sufferings were the 'glory' of his readers may
> seem strange at first, but Paul viewed his imprisonment as part of his
> service for Christ, a service that exalted the Gentiles. If he was in prison
> for preaching to the Gentiles, someone was fighting for them, and
> their position was being given attention (Rom. 11:13; Phil. 1:12-30;
> Col. 1:24-27). That he was in prison should not be discouraging.
> The discouraging thing would be that no one was willing to go to prison
> for ministry to the Gentiles.[4]

32. Read the following verses. Next to each one, write down Paul's stated
    ministry priorities.

   ◆   Romans 11:13

   ◆   Philippians 1:12-20

   ◆   Colossians 1:24-27

Paul isn't focused on the Gentiles because it is bringing him renown, but because he has been called by God to have this focus. As he moves toward the orthopraxy portion of Ephesians, he wants his Gentile readers to understand that they, too, are rooted in the promises of God—that their fruit, too comes from being part of the family of God.

Reflect

Using Ephesians 3:8-13 as a guide, write out your own declaration of gospel ministry. Pray over God's work in and through you. Then write a statement that reflects who you are in Christ and how He has called you to be at work for Him in your current season of life. Borrow as many phrases from Paul as you need to as you craft this reminder of your personal ministry.

EPHESIANS 3:14-21

Memory Verse: Now to him who is able to do above and beyond all that we ask or think according to the power that works in us—to him be glory in the church and in Christ Jesus to all generations, forever and ever. Amen.

Ephesians 3:20-21

ROOTED AND GROUNDED IN LOVE

Read through all of Ephesians 3 again. Then read Ephesians 3:1 and Ephesians 3:14-21, skipping over verses 2-13.

I am writing the days of this study in fits and starts. My boys are home from school for the summer, and as much as I plan for quiet moments and pockets of time, they find a way to jump in and interrupt me midway through a thought or a rabbit trail. I've read Ephesians while Kidz Bop® is blasting in the next room, read Ephesians while *Trolls* is playing on the screen right next to me, read Ephesians while a toddler hangs on my legs demanding my attention.

While I don't think Paul had distractions in the same sense that I do—especially while being divinely inspired to pen the God-breathed words of his epistle—most agree that Ephesians 3:2-13 was a tangent from the original prayer he was getting ready to pray in Ephesians 3:1. Ephesians 3:2-13 seems to be a digression (a worthwhile one, of course) from his original train of thought.

33. **Compare Ephesians 3:14-15 with Ephesians 3:1. How might you write Ephesians 3:1 and Ephesians 3:14-15 as one unbroken thought?**

In Ephesians 3:1, Paul reminds his readers who he is, where he is, and what his mission is. He belongs to Christ, he is in prison, and his mission is to proclaim the gospel to the Gentiles. In Ephesians 3:14-15, he's gearing up to remind his readers of who they are by describing whose they are. He is also introducing a prayer—bowing his knees before the Father—and poising himself for supplication on behalf of his readers.

34. Now read Ephesians 3:16-19. What is Paul praying for? What does Paul want his readers to be rooted in? What does he want them to comprehend?

35. Find any references to the Trinity in Ephesians 3:14-21 and note your observations in the chart.

God the Father	God the Son	God the Spirit

Circle the places you see abundance language in this passage (pp. 78-79).

This is not the first time Paul has shared details of his prayers on behalf of the Ephesian saints, but in keeping with the pattern of this letter, Paul's prayer echoes the shift from orthodoxy to orthopraxy we've been following. The first prayer (1:15-23) was about believing who God is. This prayer in chapter 3 highlights how they are to live in light of who God is—empowered by the Spirit, through faith in the Son, and filled with the fullness of the Father (3:16-19).

36. Now read 1 Corinthians 2:6-16. Focus on verses 12-13 and verse 16, which are included here. Underline where you see mention of each Person of the Trinity in this passage.

> [12]Now we have received not the spirit of the world, but the Spirit who is from God, that we might understand the things freely given us by God. [13]And we impart this in words not taught by human wisdom but taught by the Spirit, interpreting spiritual truths to those who are spiritual.
>
> [16]"For who has understood the mind of the Lord so as to instruct him?" But we have the mind of Christ (ESV).

From these passages in Ephesians 3 and 1 Corinthians 2, it is evident that Paul wanted to show how the Godhead is working together to redeem, sanctify, and inevitably glorify his readers. Paul has already told us in Ephesians 1:13 that we are sealed with the promise of the Holy Spirit, that the unbreakable bond of the Father, Son, and Spirit guarantees our salvation, with the Holy Spirit being the down payment of the inheritance purchased by Christ's sacrifice until we are in heaven with God.

There is no stronger seal.

When Paul hearkens back to that seal, that bond of the Spirit, in Ephesians 3 and 1 Corinthians 2, Paul is letting us know that we have access to the fullness of God.

We are not going to delve into the complexity of Trinitarian theology here but, suffice it to say, it is *vital* that we understand God in three Persons who are working together to bring about our salvation and the fruit of that salvation.

Remember, we are still talking about *orthodoxy* here—right belief. But *orthopraxy*—right practice—is coming around the bend. In preparation for his teaching on how to live out the faith, Paul is cementing our identity in who we are in God the Father, God the Son, and God the Holy Spirit. He is reminding us that we are rooted in their eternal, unbreakable oneness.

Paul also speaks to love twice in this prayer—first, that we be grounded in love (v. 17), and second, that we know the love of Christ that surpasses knowledge (v. 19). On the precipice of telling us how we walk out our faith, Paul reminds us what the root of that "walking out" should be: *love*.

37. **Hearken back to Paul's past as a Pharisee (Acts 7–9). Was Paul motivated by love as Saul the persecutor? How do we know?**

38. **What is the difference between Paul's focus before conversion and Paul's focus after conversion?**

Christ's love radically altered Paul's life and mission. His passion and zeal remained unmatched, but his focus shifted from persecuting those who follow Christ to risking his own life on behalf of the gospel. He would go on to tell readers (us) how Christ's love will radically alter our lives and mission, too. But before he gets into "do this" and "don't do this," he prays that we would be reminded of the why—of the root—of who we are. He prays that we will be rooted in and reminded of the love of Christ.

The love of Christ doesn't move us to stand still or stagnate; it moves us to growth, to action, to radical change. Paul is laying the foundation for that radical change by reminding us of the seed of both change and identity: Christ's love.

39. **Look again at Ephesians 3:17. In your own words, what does it mean to be rooted in Christ's love? What is the fruit of being rooted in Christ's love? How can we have access to Christ's love?**

John Stott wrote of verse 17,

> [I]n the new and reconciled humanity which Christ is creating love is the pre-eminent virtue. The new humanity is God's family, whose members are brothers and sisters, who love their Father and love each other. Or should do. They need the power of the Spirit's might and of Christ's indwelling to enable them to love each other, especially across the deep racial and cultural divide which previously had separated them. . . . To express how fundamental Paul longs for their love to be, he joins two metaphors (one botanical, the other architectural), both of which emphasize depth as opposed to superficiality . . . In both cases the unseen cause of their stability will be the same: love. Love is to be the soil in which their life is to be rooted; love is to be the foundation on which their life is built.[5]

Paul wanted his readers to be overwhelmed by the abundance of Christ's love—a love which surpasses knowledge. Yet even though that love surpasses knowledge, Paul invites us to continue to try to plumb its limitless depths. He invites us to continue trying to fathom the unfathomable. And this invitation is the same for you and me today. Before he moves us toward benediction, Paul reminds us why we're here: the love of God, exhibited to us through the Father, Son, and Spirit. And he invites us to bask in that love.

Reflect

Paul invites us to learn more about Christ's love, even though we can't possibly understand the full extent of it. Spend a few minutes reflecting on how your appreciation for Jesus has grown and developed throughout your walk with Him. Write down any thoughts you have as you recall the love Christ has for you.

We should never stop being amazed by the love of Christ. How can this practice of remembering continue to transform our understanding of Christ's love for us? What is a practical, specific way you can dwell on the love of Christ more every day?

TO HIM WHO IS ABLE

Read all of Ephesians 3 once more. Then reread
Ephesians 3:20-21.

Readers who have spent time in the church might recognize
the words at the end of Ephesians 3 as a benediction. Pastor
H.B. Charles describes a benediction as follows:

> Many Christian worship services end with a benediction.
> A benediction is simply a blessing. Pastors have the
> privilege of announcing, prayerfully, divine blessings
> on the people of God as they scatter from the place of
> corporate worship. The benediction is often announced
> simply by quoting the Scriptures.[6]

40. **Read three of Paul's benedictions that we find in his
New Testament letters. Restate each benediction in your
own words,**

> *Now may the God of hope fill you with all joy and
> peace as you believe so that you may overflow
> with hope by the power of the Holy Spirit.*

   ROMANS 15:13

   Restate:

> *The grace of the Lord Jesus Christ, and
> the love of God, and the fellowship of
> the Holy Spirit be with you all.*

   2 CORINTHIANS 13:13

   Restate:

EPHESIANS 3:20-21

Memory Verse: Now
to him who is able to
do above and beyond
all that we ask or
think according to the
power that works in
us—to him be glory
in the church and
in Christ Jesus to all
generations, forever
and ever. Amen.
Ephesians 3:20-21

*Now to him who is able to do above and beyond all
that we ask or think according to the power that works
in us—to him be glory in the church and in Christ
Jesus to all generations, forever and ever. Amen.*

EPHESIANS 3:20-21

Restate:

41. What is similar about these benedictions?

42. What is different about them?

43. What stands out to you from the benediction to the Ephesians?

Paul's benediction to the Ephesians is notably lengthier than the previous two benedictions, and you may have also noticed his mention of "the church." One helpful distinction here is that Ephesians 3:20-21 is functioning as both a *benediction* and a *doxology*. H.B. Charles is helpful again here:

> *A doxology in scripture is a statement of praise. It is a declaration of praise. It is used many times in the writings of the epistles and the letters. And particularly Paul uses them often in the middle of some important theological statement he makes that he moves from theology to doxology. Which truly is the purpose of right theology. Right theology ought to lead to high doxology. A right thinking about God ought to lead to a right worship of God.[7]*

44. **How is a benediction different from a doxology? How are they similar? Where is the overlap?**

With these words in Ephesians 3:20-21, Paul is speaking divine blessing over the congregation and making a statement of praise towards God. H.B. Charles describes this pause for praise as "a bridge between doctrine and duty."[8] Does that statement remind you of anything? At the beginning of this week, we talked about the fact that Ephesians is divided into two sections: Ephesians 1–3 focuses on *orthodoxy* while Ephesians 4–6 focuses on *orthopraxy*.

45. **Remember:**

◆ **Orthodoxy is**

◆ **Orthopraxy is**

But Paul doesn't jump straight from orthodoxy into orthopraxy. As he enumerates the goodness of God in what we are called to believe about Christ, he pauses to praise God and to bless his listeners. He pauses to give a benediction and a prayer, signaling his first response to the goodness of God—praise—and his transition to a second response to the goodness of God—obedience.

Paul's doxology in verses 20-21 is the letter's bridge between doctrine and duty. He is reminding us of God's incredible blessing toward us, and he is praising God for His incredible blessing toward us. Both things are happening at the same time in a beautiful crescendo of praise to God.

One distinct feature I don't want you to miss about this benediction is Paul's mention of the church. In the midst of his praise for all that God is for His people, Paul says: "to him be the glory in the church and in Christ Jesus." This is an important reminder for readers of "the unending relationship between God, his people, and Christ."[9]

46. **Reread Ephesians 3:21. How has Paul woven the three members of the Godhead into this text? Who are they? What are the things he has described them doing?**

Remember, earlier in his prayer, Paul made sure to include every Person of the Godhead as a nod to the fact that the Father, Son, and Holy Spirit work together in procuring our salvation and sealing us for eternity. Paul continues to remind us that this work has been accomplished through the Father, Son, and Holy Spirit on behalf of a people who have been sustained by Him in all of His fullness. We glorify God in our worship of Him as we are included into the church.

And we do this throughout all generations, forever and ever. Paul points out that we will have an eternity in heaven worshiping God in all of His fullness. In doing so, he reminds us that our salvation is assured *forever*—we are sealed *forever*, and we are in relationship with God *forever*—be we Jew or Gentile.

With that, Paul closes his prayer with a hearty amen, moving forward toward the result of this praise and this standing with God—a life of obedience.

But before we get to Ephesians 4, take stock of the orthodoxy that we have learned in chapters 1–3. Look back through your study notes and the chapters of Paul's letter as you consider the following review questions.

47. What has Paul taught us about:

God the Father	God the Son	God the Spirit

48. What has Paul taught us about our salvation?

49. What is the mystery that he has revealed?

50. Before we move on, I also want you to focus on the language of abundance in Ephesians 3:20-21. It's there. (Circle) it in the text.

As we move toward obedience, we are not drawing from an empty well. We are deeply rooted in the abundant love of our Savior and the abundant goodness of God, and we are sealed by the unbreakable power of the Holy Spirit. Paul has laid this groundwork for us to know who God is and who we are in Him. He has pointed to our unshakable foundation.

Now, let's build!

Reflect

Before you wrap-up this week's study, take some time to reflect on these questions:

What did you learn about God the Father, God the Son, and God the Holy Spirit in Ephesians 3?

....

....

....

What did you learn about your relationship with God? Who are you in light of who He is and how He is at work?

....

....

....

How is God challenging you to live transformed by the power of His Word?

....

....

....

....

Now to him who is able to do above and beyond all that we ask or think according to the power that works in us—to him be glory in the church and in Christ Jesus to all generations, forever and ever. Amen.

EPHESIANS 3:20-21

WATCH

Watch the Session Four video and take notes below.

TO ACCESS THE VIDEO SESSIONS, USE THE INSTRUCTIONS
IN THE BACK OF YOUR BIBLE STUDY BOOK.

DISCUSS

1. Which day of personal study had the most impact on you, and why? What lingering questions do you have?

2. How did what you heard on the video clarify, reinforce, or give new insight to what you studied this session?

3. When you think about Paul's personal ministry—from who he was before he met Jesus to how God used him after—how are you encouraged or challenged in your own ministry? How might Paul's example transform your feelings of shame, unworthiness, or arrogance?

4. How do you want to live differently in the week to come because of what we've studied this week?

5. Use Paul's prayer for spiritual power in Ephesians 3:14-21 as a model for your group's prayer time today.

EPHESIANS 4

UNITY & MATURITY

This week, our focus shifts from orthodoxy (who God is) to orthopraxy (what He expects of us). Paul has shown us that we serve a loving God full of abundant blessings. A God who has enfolded both Jews and Gentiles into His family and loves us all as sons and daughters. A God who has sealed our place in His family with the sacrifice of the Son and the guarantee of the Spirit. Paul has shown us that God is good. He's set God's goodness as the groundwork for our obedience to Him. Now we'll start to unpack how we can show our devotion to our loving God.

Jasmine

EPHESIANS 4

UNITY AND DIVERSITY IN THE BODY OF CHRIST

Therefore I, the prisoner in the Lord, urge you to walk worthy of the calling you have received, ² with all humility and gentleness, with patience, bearing with one another in love, ³ making every effort to keep the unity of the Spirit through the bond of peace. ⁴ There is one body and one Spirit—just as you were called to one hope at your calling— ⁵ one Lord, one faith, one baptism, ⁶ one God and Father of all, who is above all and through all and in all.

⁷ Now grace was given to each one of us according to the measure of Christ's gift. ⁸ For it says:

When he ascended on high,
he took the captives captive;
he gave gifts to people.

⁹ But what does "he ascended" mean except that he also descended to the lower parts of the earth? ¹⁰ The one who descended is also the one who ascended far above all the heavens, to fill all things. ¹¹ And he himself gave some to be apostles, some prophets, some evangelists, some pastors and teachers, ¹² to equip the saints for the work of ministry, to build up the body of Christ, ¹³ until we all reach unity in the faith and in the knowledge of God's Son, growing into maturity with a stature measured by Christ's fullness. ¹⁴ Then

we will no longer be little children, tossed by the waves and blown around by every wind of teaching, by human cunning with cleverness in the techniques of deceit. [15] But speaking the truth in love, let us grow in every way into him who is the head—Christ. [16] From him the whole body, fitted and knit together by every supporting ligament, promotes the growth of the body for building itself up in love by the proper working of each individual part.

LIVING THE NEW LIFE

[17] Therefore, I say this and testify in the Lord: You should no longer walk as the Gentiles do, in the futility of their thoughts. [18] They are darkened in their understanding, excluded from the life of God, because of the ignorance that is in them and because of the hardness of their hearts. [19] They became callous and gave themselves over to promiscuity for the practice of every kind of impurity with a desire for more and more.

[20] But that is not how you came to know Christ, [21] assuming you heard about him and were taught by him, as the truth is in Jesus, [22] to take off your former way of life, the old self that is corrupted by deceitful desires, [23] to be renewed in the spirit of your minds, [24] and to put on the new self, the one created according to God's likeness in righteousness and purity of the truth.

[25] Therefore, putting away lying, speak the truth, each one to his neighbor, because we are members of one another. [26] Be angry and do not sin. Don't let the sun go down on your anger, [27] and don't give the devil an opportunity. [28] Let the thief no longer steal. Instead, he is to do honest work with his own hands, so that he has something to share with anyone in need. [29] No foul language should come from your mouth, but only what is good for building up someone in need, so that it gives grace to those who hear. [30] And don't grieve God's Holy Spirit. You were sealed by him for the day of redemption. [31] Let all bitterness, anger and wrath, shouting and slander be removed from you, along with all malice. [32] And be kind and compassionate to one another, forgiving one another, just as God also forgave you in Christ.

EPHESIANS 4

Memory Verse:

Therefore I, the prisoner in the Lord, urge you to walk worthy of the calling you have received.

Ephesians 4:1

BEARING FRUIT

Read Ephesians 4–6 in full.

With Paul's "therefore" at the start of Ephesians 4, we've officially transitioned into the second half of the book of Ephesians. We're halfway to the finish line, but can you believe how much ground Paul has already covered? In just three short chapters, Paul has taught on some of the most profound and important truths of the Christian faith. He has laid the groundwork for who we are to be by teaching us who God is. We've dug the roots of orthodoxy deep into the fertile soil of God's Word and now it's time to start bearing fruit.

1. **Review what you learned in the first three chapters. Pick three major concepts that Paul laid out for his readers and note them below. Focus on each chapter in turn.**

    ◆   Ephesians 1

    ◆   Ephesians 2

    ◆   Ephesians 3

2. **In the previous session, we looked at Luke 6:43-45 and Matthew 12:33-37, where Jesus reminds us that a tree is known by its fruit (pp. 80-81). Read those passages again to review Jesus's teaching.**

3. **Now read John 15:1-11. After you've read the full passage, focus in on verses 4-8, which are printed below. As you read, <u>underline</u> the vine and fruit metaphor wherever you see it. And look, once more, for the language of abundance.**

> *Abide in me, and I in you. As the branch cannot bear fruit by itself, unless it abides in the vine, neither can you, unless you abide in me. I am the vine; you are the branches. Whoever abides in me and I in him, he it is that bears much fruit, for apart from me you can do nothing. If anyone does not abide in me he is thrown away like a branch and withers; and the branches are gathered, thrown into the fire, and burned. If you abide in me, and my words abide in you, ask whatever you wish, and it will be done for you. By this my Father is glorified, that you bear much fruit and so prove to be my disciples.*
>
> JOHN 15:4-8, ESV

4. **Look up the definition of the word *abide* and write it here.**

ABIDE

5. **What happens when we abide in Christ? What about when we do not abide in Him?**

For the last three chapters, Paul has been describing exactly what it is to abide in Christ. He has been showing us where our home is, building from the foundation up. He has rooted us in the triune God and grounded us in our place in His family. He has built his case seamlessly, overflowing with praise at the timeless truths he has taught us.

Through it all, Paul is communicating the change that he himself has experienced.

6. **Read Galatians 1:11-17, where Paul gives his testimony. Pay close attention to the order of events. Put the following events in the correct order:**

_____ Paul is radically changed.

_____ People glorify God because of Paul.

_____ Paul persecutes the church.

_____ Paul meets Jesus.

_____ Paul is called by God.

_____ Paul begins to preach.

Paul did not meet Jesus on the road to Damascus in Acts 9 and instantaneously change into the man who wrote the epistles we know so well. He spent time being discipled, learning more about Christ, and learning to abide in Him. He spent three years studying and growing with Jesus before transitioning into a life of ministry. He fully understood the truth of the gospel that he had been called to proclaim, and it did its changing work in him in time.

Paul illustrates that time through the first three chapters of Ephesians. He is writing this letter to the believers in Ephesus so that they might:

1. **Gain greater understanding into the fullness of God's truth, and**

2. **Walk in obedience because of that understanding.**

The second cannot happen without the first.

7. **Ephesians 4–6 presents us with a lot of things to do. Do you remember some of them from your reading? Jot a few down below.**

8. **But let's also remember that Ephesians 1–3 presents us with who we are and whose we are. Do you remember some of those moments? Write them below.**

Ephesians 1–3 has been an invitation to abide in Christ by the grace of God through the Spirit of God. Ephesians 4–6 tells us what the result of that abiding will be: we will bear fruit. Paul echoes the teachings of Jesus here.

> *Abide in me, and I in you. As the branch cannot bear fruit by itself, unless it abides in the vine, neither can you, unless you abide in me.*

JOHN 15:4, ESV

I'm far beyond my elementary school days, but you'd better believe that I can still recite PEMDAS with the rest of them: Please Excuse My Dear Aunt Sally. It's the order of operations, the code that makes more complex math problems click. Math is a universal language, and PEMDAS is one of our first translation guides: Parentheses, Exponents, Multiplication and Division, Addition and Subtraction (from left to right). The problem won't make sense if we add before we've dealt with exponents; if we ignore parentheses and work things out in spite of them; if we decide we want to work from right to left.

Paul's order of operations is even more important. *We can't delight in obeying the Lord if we don't know Him.* We have to learn His name—to begin to plumb the depths of the fullness and goodness and love that God offers—before we can bring honor to that name through our obedience to Him.

This is not to say that Paul is done drawing our eyes to God and His goodness. Far from it. Because even as we move towards obedience, we need to be reminded of where our rootedness lies. Our obedience is not an end unto itself: we live lives worthy of our callings *because* of the love that has been displayed toward us, and *because* of the love we have in turn.

Reflect

Jesus invites you to abide in Him. Before we mine through Paul's practical teachings on life in Christ, sit in the fullness of that invitation. Read back over John 15:1-11 and everything Jesus says to you there. List those things out. Highlight the ones you most needed to be reminded of today.

DAY TWO
2

EPHESIANS 4:1-6

Memory Verse:

Therefore I, the prisoner in the Lord, urge you to walk worthy of the calling you have received.

Ephesians 4:1

LOVE AND UNITY

Read Ephesians 4. Now go back and read 4:1-6 again, aloud if you're able.

In his introduction to Ephesians 4, Klyne Snodgrass states:

Throughout the New Testament, ethical imperatives are based on theological indicatives. Obedience is always a response to grace. God acts first, and humans respond. Just as kerygma (proclamation) and didache (instruction) cannot be separated, neither can the indicative and the imperative. The two blend together in the same text. The imperative can be a means of preaching the gospel, for ethical statements can contain the whole gospel.[1]

9. **Summarize Snodgrass's point in your own words below.**

As we get our bearings in Ephesians 4, it's important to remember that emphasizing the response to grace doesn't mean we've completely left behind Paul's reminders of the foundational grace in Ephesians 1–3. It's still woven throughout this chapter. But we see a definite tonal shift.

10. **Read Ephesians 4:1-3 (p. 112). Circle the first clause before the comma.**

11. **Why does Paul call himself a "prisoner in the Lord"?**

12. **What is the calling to which the Ephesians have been called?**

13. **List the virtues that Paul wants the church to maintain.**

Those first words you circled, "Therefore I," hearken back to the foundation that Paul has been laying throughout this book. In light of who Christ is and what He has done for us, here are the next steps. In light of our deep rootedness in the unity of the Godhead, here's what needs to happen next.

Paul's exhortation in verses 2-3 would sound very familiar to my second grader, who has been singing, "The fruit of the Spirit's not a coconut," for several years now.[2]

Read Galatians 5:16-24. We are going to hone in on verses 22-24 here, but we will return to the passage as a whole later this week.

14. **Below, <u>underline</u> the fruit of the Spirit that are echoed in Ephesians 4:2-3.**

But the fruit of the Spirit is love, joy, peace, patience, kindness, goodness, faithfulness, gentleness, and self-control. The law is not against such things. Now those who belong to Christ Jesus have crucified the flesh with its passions and desires.

GALATIANS 5:22-24

15. **What verse in Ephesians 4 do the above verses in Galatians 5 remind you of?**

16. **Why do you think Paul chooses to emphasize humility, gentleness, patience, love, and unity in Ephesians 4:2-3? Use what you've learned about the church in Ephesus to help you answer.**

17. **Where do we see unity in Galatians 5?**

The fruit of the Spirit is *the fruit of the Spirit*—the indwelling Spirit we've been talking about throughout Ephesians. The same Spirit who is the guarantor of our salvation (Eph. 1:14) works in us to produce the fruit that Paul wants to see. The Spirit is in perfect unity with Son and Father, and through our unity with the Spirit—this bond of peace—we are able to produce the fruit of that unity. Snodgrass's teaching is so helpful here:

> *The English imperatives that follow in 4:2-3 are actually prepositional phrases ("with all humility," etc.) and participles ("bearing . . . making every effort"). This is not a series of imperatives of equal rank. Even if the phrases in verses 2–3 are understood imperatively, they are subordinate to the one main imperative—"live worthy of the calling you have received." They describe a life worthy of God's calling, which is marked by humility, gentleness, patience, tolerant love, and peacekeeping. Attention goes first to the ego and then to loving relations. An understanding of God's work is always an attack on the ego, not to obliterate or humiliate the self, but to bring it into relation with God and to redirect its interests. In losing life we find it.[3]*

18. Read Ephesians 4:4-6 (p. 112). Circle the word *one* every time you see it. Below, write down all of the ones that Paul points out in this passage.

 ◆ One _____

 ◆ One _____

 ◆ One _____

 ◆ One _____

 ◆ One _____

 ◆ One _____

 ◆ One _____

Again, we see the theological foundation that Paul has laid for us leading up to this next section. Here he hearkens back to several statements he's already made in this letter.

19. **Read each passage listed below. Next to each reference, list out the phrases that remind you of Ephesians 4:4-6.**

    ◆ **Ephesians 2:14-18**

    ◆ **Ephesians 2:21-22**

    ◆ **Ephesians 3:6**

Paul spent a great deal of Ephesians 3 letting us know that Gentiles are included in his salvation message. Now, in chapter 4, he's hammering home the idea that we are one family. Surely, this is not coincidental. Paul has told us what the Lord requires of us in Ephesians 4:1-3. Now, in Ephesians 4:4-6, he is telling us both *why* it is required of us and *how* we will accomplish it.

20. **Why is unity required of the church?**

    How does Paul say we will accomplish that unity?

    Why is this message of unity particularly impactful coming from Paul?

Paul knows this task will not be easy. Later on, he is going to tell us exactly the kind of unity and love in action that he expects from believers. And in other epistles, he is going to tell other churches where they are failing miserably. Even with all of the theological groundwork laid, we still struggle with the most basic display of our unity: love.

One verse from another of Paul's letters comes to mind as we continue to unfold the beautiful truths Paul is teaching us. Consider his words to the church in Corinth:

> *If I have the gift of prophecy and understand all mysteries and all knowledge, and if I have all faith so that I can move mountains but do not have love, I am nothing.*

1 CORINTHIANS 13:2

Paul says that if we "understand all mysteries and all knowledge" but don't have love, we are "nothing."

Paul has been enumerating upon the knowledge of the fullness of God in his letter to the Ephesians. He has uncovered mysteries imparted to him by the Divine. But here, in chapter 4, Paul stops to remind us that if these truths don't move us towards a greater love of God and unity with the people whom He loves, we've misunderstood the very foundation of our faith.

Reflect ———

Write down what love is according to 1 Corinthians 13.

Write down how Ephesians 4:4 moves you toward greater love.

Spend a few minutes in prayer, reflecting on the love Jesus has shown you and the love you're called to show others. What has God impressed on you through your study today?

UNITY IN DIVERSITY

Read Ephesians 4 from a translation other than the one you've been reading.

Paul has already set the faith in practice bar high in the first few verses of Ephesians 4. He's reminded us of our lofty calling—one marked by humility, gentleness, patience, love, and unity. And, once again, he's cemented that unity into the reality of the triune God "who is over all and through all and in all" (v. 6).

Memory Verse:

Therefore I, the prisoner in the Lord, urge you to walk worthy of the calling you have received.

Ephesians 4:1

21. **Now I want you to read Ephesians 4:7-16 a few times.**

   ◆ **First, read verses 7-16 straight through.**

   ◆ **Next, read the passage again, but this time read it aloud and skip over verses 9 and 10.**

   ◆ **Then, read it all together one more time.**

On the heels of his call to love and unity, Paul stops here to make an important distinction: unity does not equal uniformity. The gifts Jesus gives His followers thrive in diversity. Verse 7 puts it this way: "grace was given to each one of us [underline those words in your copy of the text] according to the measure of Christ's gift." Christ wants us to strive for unity in the body, and He accomplishes that unity by giving us all individual gifts with which to glorify Him and serve others.

22. **Read the following verses. (You'll want to bookmark them too, we're coming back to them.)**

   ◆ Romans 12:3-8. **Write verse 4 below.**

   ◆ 1 Corinthians 12:4-14. **Write verses 4-6 below.**

Now hold that thought while we follow one of Paul's tangential remarks. In Ephesians 4:8, Paul references Psalm 68:18 in making his point: "You ascended to the heights, taking away captives; you received gifts from people, even from the rebellious, so that the Lord God might dwell there."

23. **What do you make of this connection between Jesus's ascension to heaven and the spiritual gifts you have in Him?**

I love what the Africa Bible Commentary says about this part of the text: "Paul quotes Psalm 68:18, implying that these gifts are like rewards that a victorious general distributes to his supporters, who may not have even been present at the battle."[4] What a picture! Christ has accomplished victory over sin and death, and He gives us gifts fitted to the unique way He made us and the unique calling He has on our lives. More specifically, He gives us as gifts to His church.

In Ephesians 4:8-10, Paul diverts his attention for a moment to a parenthetical notation that has the capacity to throw us into a tailspin. Verses 9 and 10 talk about Christ descending into the "lower regions of the earth" and then ascending "far above the heavens." There are a handful of different ways to interpret this passage, including that Christ descended into hell itself. Three other possible interpretations are:

- Christ's incarnation;

- Christ's descent in the Spirit at Pentecost;

- Christ's descent to the church alluded to in 2:17.

Rather than land definitively on one of these interpretations, I will state that the most important element of this parenthetical notation is that it refers in some way to Jesus's humility in the incarnation and His ultimate glory over all things.

Moving to Ephesians 4:11-16, we see two things: (1) a short list of giftings that God has given to serve the body, and (2) what Paul hopes these gifted ones will equip the saints to do.

24. Look back over Romans 12:3-8; 1 Corinthians 12:4-14; and Ephesians 4:11-12. Write down some of the specific gifts Paul mentions in these passages.

What stands out to you as you examine these lists?

We know from other passages about gifts that Paul does not think only apostles, prophets, evangelists, shepherds, and teachers are being used by God for His glory. And it's helpful to remember that none of the spiritual gifts lists in Scripture are exhaustive. But Paul does home in on key gifts here that relate to teaching the Word of God and leading the body of Christ, as well as the lessons that he wants them to be teaching.

25. List the things Paul wants to equip the saints to do (look for the word *for*).

26. Paul desires unity of faith and the knowledge of the Son of God, but to what end? Read verses 13-14. Write Paul's end goal below.

Paul does not want us to stagnate, but rather to continue growing "to the measure of the stature of the fullness of Christ." He shows us that the opposite of immaturity is to speak the truth in love and to grow into

Christlikeness. One of the primary responsibilities of those gifted to teach and lead in the church is to see this work through in the lives of their church members.

Again, Paul reminds us here that we are one body (v. 13). Remember in verse 4, Paul really drives home the message of unity and oneness. He has stopped to clarify that this unity does not mean uniformity – but it does mean growth together in love.

27. **Pause and circle the language of abundance in today's passage (pp. 112-113). Look for words like *fullness* and *every* and *equipped* and *all*.**

Paul tells us about God's desire for us while also equipping us with the means to fulfill that desire. He's given us everything we need to thrive—proverbial sunlight, water, nutrient rich soil, healthy root system—and tells us to grow instead of wither. To thrive instead of to stagnate. We have, in abundance, everything that we need to thrive and grow in Christ.

That doesn't mean it's easy. If it were, I doubt Paul would have taken such pains to exhort the church in so many ways: we'd just have to give our lives to Christ and trust instinct to kick in and take care of the rest. Instead, God has given us the body of Christ and myriad unique giftings to help us in this process of growth.

As it turns out, we aren't many trees in a forest, but one tree. Our unity and growth contribute to the health of the entire unit. There is strength in our numbers, too. We are less vulnerable to deceit when we learn and thrive in the community that God has given us.

28. **Why do you think that Paul keeps returning to love in this chapter?**

Paul remembered what is so easy for us to forget: It is impossible to "walk worthy of the calling you have received" apart from love—God's love for you and the overflow of His love through you toward others. In Stott's words,

> The apostle sets before us the picture of a deepening fellowship, an eagerness to maintain visible Christian unity and to recover if it is lost, an active every-member ministry and a steady growth into maturity by holding the truth in love. We need to keep this biblical ideal clearly before us. Only then shall we live a life that is worthy of it.[5]

Reflect ———

Look back over today's Ephesians passage and study. What is one thing you've learned that you need to live out today?

Spend a few moments in prayer. Voice a prayer of gratitude to Jesus for the love He has shown you. Ask Him to help you keep love front and center today as you live out your calling.

EPHESIANS 4:17-24

Memory Verse:

Therefore I, the prisoner in the Lord, urge you to walk worthy of the calling you have received.

Ephesians 4:1

THEN & NOW

Read or listen to Ephesians 4. Now go back and reread Ephesians 4:17-24.

Today, we're diving into a theme that will carry us through the rest of Ephesians 4—contrast. This is not the first time Paul has used contrasts to help make his points in Ephesians.

29. **Read Ephesians 2:1-5; 2:11-13; 2:19; and 5:8.**
    In the table below, fill in the "now" halves of the then and now contrasts that Paul lays out in these passages:

Then	Now
Ephesians 2:1—you were dead in your trespasses	Ephesians 2:5—you are . . .
Ephesians 2:11-12—you were Gentiles in the flesh, separated from Christ	Ephesians 2:13—you are . . .
Ephesians 2:19—you were strangers and aliens	Ephesians 2:19—you are . . .
Ephesians 4:18—you were darkened in your understanding	Ephesians 4:23—you are . . .
Ephesians 5:8—you were darkness	Ephesians 5:8—you are . . .

Paul hasn't laid out the glorious groundwork thus far in Ephesians for us to just stay exactly as we are. This should be good news, but if we're honest it might rub us the wrong way. Because don't we want to be loved *exactly* as we are?

Here's the beauty of the gospel: God did not wait until we looked like the right column to save us. He plucked us out of death's grasp when the left column was our identity—dead, separated, strangers, darkened in our understanding, darkness itself.

Paul didn't bury the lead here. He told us back in 2:10 where this was going.

> *For we are his workmanship, created in Christ Jesus for good*
> *works, which God prepared ahead of time for us to do.*
>
> **EPHESIANS 2:10**

30. **Who created us? For what purpose? When was our purpose set?**

There's so much beauty here. Sin has affected everything about the world we live in—creation groans for the return of Christ (Rom. 8:22), and we are part of creation. Our sinful nature is indicative of the fact that something is amiss.

I'm reminded of the character Ms. Clavel from the children's book *Madeline* sitting bolt upright in bed and knowing, deep down, that "Something is not right!"[6] The transforming power of Christ—the abundance that we've been talking about throughout the book of Ephesians—starts the work of making things right.

Verse 17 might feel jolting after chapter 3—didn't Paul *just* say that the Gentiles are now included into the family of faith? Where is all of this shade coming from? But remember who Paul was before conversion?

31. **Go back and read Acts 8:1-3 for a refresher. Who was he?**

32. Now look at the ways Paul describes the life of the Gentiles in verses 17-21. How does Paul describe "living like a Gentile"? What are the characteristics?

33. How many of those characteristics can we see in Paul, pre-conversion, in Acts 8?

34. How does the idea of "impurity" contrast with the abundance language we've been paying attention to in the last two chapters?

Paul is not speaking ill of the Gentiles ethnically; rather, he is pointing out that, apart from saving faith in Christ, we are all inclined to act like the Gentiles, with *Gentile* here referring to anyone not part of the family of faith. He's reminding his listeners that they have been brought into the fold – that they have a new, transformative allegiance to Christ. Jews and Gentiles alike are called to live like Christ. Jews and Gentiles alike can fall short of doing so. And now that the family of God extends beyond the Jews who were its first focus, Paul is pointing out that there's an entirely new category: Christians. Followers of The Way.

"No longer walk as the Gentiles do" doesn't mean "walk like the Jewish people do." It means, "Walk as Christ does." Just in case that's not crystal clear enough for us, we can flip back just a few pages to Galatians and see Paul laying into the legalism of his Jewish brethren as well.

35. Read Galatians 3:7-9. Who does Paul say are the sons of Abraham?

36. **Are the Gentiles justified by their lineage? If not, what are they justified by?**

Are the Jews justified by their lineage? If not, what are they justified by?

After a brief time in existence, the church in Galatia faced issues that centered around their temptation to fall back into their Jewish traditions, namely the practice of circumcision. To a group of Christians who were trying to mandate the traditional Jewish practice, Paul reminded them that before God appointed Abraham the father of His chosen people, Abraham himself was a "Gentile" who was saved only by his faith in the One True God.

Reread Ephesians 4:22-24.

Here Paul tells us exactly how to walk as Christ does: We take off our old self and put on the new self, "created according to God's likeness in righteousness and purity of the truth." This "take off" and "put on" language is going to extend into the rest of the chapter, complete with examples. But, for today, let's note that none of this taking off and putting on is what saves us.

Paul has already told us exactly what (who) saves us. He has given us the clearest possible picture of the abundant love offered to us in Christ Jesus. The changes he is advocating for are *the result* of saving faith, not its prerequisite. They are an outpouring of having a mind renewed by Christ. That doesn't mean that they're easy—our flesh is still something we war with every day. But change and growth is an inevitable result of walking with Jesus. For the Jew first, and also, the Gentile.

Reflect ——————————————————————

Look back at the chart you filled in at the start of today's study. Use each pair of contrasting statements as a guided prayer of praise and thanksgiving to the One who has given you new life.

DAY FIVE

5

EPHESIANS 4:25-31

Memory Verse:

Therefore I, the prisoner in the Lord, urge you to walk worthy of the calling you have received.

Ephesians 4:1

WRAP UP

Read Ephesians 4. Reread Ephesians 4:25-31.

At the beginning of Ephesians 3, we talked about the orthodoxy/orthopraxy divide in Paul's letter. Let's review:

37. **What is orthodoxy?**

    What is orthopraxy?

    Is there orthodoxy in Ephesians 4–6? (Circle one.)

    YES   NO

Up until this point, Paul has still been weaving in plenty of right belief into the second half of his letter, reminding the church exactly who Christ is as he reminds them of who they are in Christ.

38. **Recall (from memory if you can) one right belief and one right practice Paul teaches in Ephesians 4.**

    ◆   **Right belief**

    ◆   **Right practice**

    How do the two things you noted relate to each other?

In today's passage, we step all the way into the realm of the practical. Paul told us in verse 22 that we needed to put off the old self, and in verse 24 that we needed to put on the new self. In verses 25-29, he gives us examples of what we're supposed to put off and put on.

39. **Fill in the table below with what Paul tells his readers to put on, and look for any themes as you go.**

Verse 25 – put away falsehood	Verse 25 – put on . . .
Verse 28 – put away stealing	Verse 28 –
Verse 29 – put away corrupting talk	Verse 29 –
Verse 31 – put away bitterness, wrath, anger, clamor, slander, and malice	Verse 32 –

40. **Note one or two things that stand out to you from verses 25-32. Is anything surprising? What feels particularly challenging or motivating?**

41. **Write, in your own words, a one-sentence summary of Paul's instructions in this part of his letter.**

With everything he's written before this point Paul has laid the groundwork for his extremely practical instructions for the Christian life. Because of who God is and who we are in Him, the Christian is called to a way of life that models that of Jesus Himself—one marked by loving sacrifice and selflessness.

Snodgrass notes of these verses, "Some Christians worry about such specific directions for living, for they fear it may lead to legalism, but this thinking is far from the New Testament. Texts like this do not endorse legalism; they are descriptions of life in Christ, which is never without content. Christian living requires certain and specific actions. The Christian faith is not a passive religion; it is an aggressive pursuit of the productive and beneficial."[7] These are fruits that grow out of a life attached to the vine of Christ.

Did you notice how all of Paul's "put offs" have to do with our relationships to others? Lying, anger, stealing, and corrupting talk all have to do with harming other people. And Paul's "put ons" also focus on others. Why is this so important? "Because we are members of one another" (Eph. 4:25).

42. **Go back and reread Ephesians 4:1-6. How does Paul tell us to walk (v. 1)? Why does he tell us to walk this way (v. 3)?**

43. **What are the "one" statements that he makes in verses 4-5?**

Ephesians 4:25-32 is reasserting the truth that we learned earlier in the chapter: We are one in Christ, His body the church, and we should walk in a way that both illustrates and cultivates unity.

Read back over Ephesians 4:26-27, ESV.

> *Be angry and do not sin; do not let the sun go down on your anger and give no opportunity to the devil.*

These verses on anger are part of Paul's practical exhortations, but unlike his "put off" and "put on" examples, Paul does not tell his readers to do away with anger here. Paul actually tells his readers to *be angry*.

44. **What are some proper contexts you can think of for anger, instances when it would be an example of right belief?**

45. **Why do you think Paul puts a time limit on anger?**

46. What opportunity might the devil take with anger?

Paul draws out a few helpful instructions for how the Christian is to manage anger. He permits anger, making it clear that anger in and of itself is not a sin. Plenty of things in our broken world should cause us to feel anger. The danger lies in what our anger is rooted in and what we choose to do with it. Satan "knows how fine is the line between righteous and unrighteous anger, and how hard human beings find it to handle their anger responsibly. So he loves to lurk round angry people, hoping to be able to exploit the situation to his own advantage by provoking them into hatred or violence or a breach of fellowship."[8]

After returning to a few more contrasting pairs in verses 28-29, Paul emphasizes the consequence of not walking in love towards our brothers and sisters in Christ:

> *And do not grieve the Holy Spirit of God, by whom you were sealed for the day of redemption.*
>
> **EPHESIANS 4:30, ESV**

This is serious. Paul invokes a reminder of the truth he's already told us in chapter 2: We are sealed by the Holy Spirit, and that Father, Son, and Spirit work together to secure our eternity with God. There is nothing weightier for us than this truth.

> *The Holy Spirit does the work of spiritual transformation or change in us, leading us to put off the thoughts and deeds of the old self and put on those of the new self. When we act in a way that shows we are not willing to put off the old self, the Holy Spirit is grieved and disappointed. Even though the Spirit has sealed us for the day of redemption, the redemption has still to be consummated. In the intervening period, we are not to do anything that will grieve the Spirit.*[9]

Paul then closes this chapter with a reminder of exactly why we are to do these things.

*Be kind to one another, tenderhearted, forgiving one
another, just as God in Christ forgave you.*

EPHESIANS 4:32, ESV

That *just as* clause is such a potent reminder of the fact that we are trading the impulses of our flesh for the "fullness of God" (3:19). That, in the words of 1 Corinthians 2, we are trading our first mind for the very mind of Christ. We are emulating Him.

47. **Think about what you know about Jesus from the Gospel accounts of His time on earth. Write down an example that comes to mind of a time when He:**

   ◆   **Spoke the truth**

   ◆   **Was angry and did not sin**

   ◆   **Labored honestly**

   ◆   **Spoke words that built others up**

   ◆   **Did not give in to bitterness, wrath, anger, clamor, slander, or malice**

As we move into Ephesians 5, we must keep Jesus at the forefront. He is who we are emulating. He is who unites us to the people we are called to love. He is who lived a perfect life, suffered, and died so that we might be brought into the family of faith.

He is the reason we are here.

Reflect ——————————————————

Before you wrap up this week's study, take some time to reflect on these questions.

What did you learn about God in Ephesians 4?

God the Father	God the Son	God the Spirit

What did you learn about your relationship with God? Who are you in light of who He is and how He is at work?

How is God challenging you to live transformed by the power of His Word?

WATCH

Watch the Session Five video and take notes below.

TO ACCESS THE VIDEO SESSIONS, USE THE INSTRUCTIONS
IN THE BACK OF YOUR BIBLE STUDY BOOK.

DISCUSS

*Discuss the following questions with your Bible study group. A more
extensive leader guide is available for free download at*
lifeway.com/ephesiansstudy.

1 Which day of personal study had the most impact on you, and
why? What lingering questions do you have?

2 How did what you heard on the video clarify, reinforce, or give
new insight to what you studied this session?

3 How do you see the balance (or lack thereof) between unity
and diversity playing out in your church and your Christian
relationships?

4 What is particularly challenging about the way we are called to live
in Ephesians 4:17-32? What are some ways we can help each other
be more mindful of the Spirit's presence and power?

5 How do you want to live differently in the week to come because
of what we've studied this week?

LIGHT & LOVE

If I called you a saint, would you know what I meant by the term? It's neither a flattering description nor a realistic assumption if you're imagining pompous perfection. Images of men long gone, with halos overhead as if to say to all who see them, "We are the special ones." But if by saint we mean what the Spirit, through Paul, means in Ephesians, then the dance of duty and delight is made available to us.

This term saint isn't reserved for the few who walked with the risen Christ; it's applied to all the children of God (Eph. 1:1). It implies something about grace since it's an identity none of us deserve but many of us have received. And, by virtue of said grace, our halos aren't above us but proven through us. Which is to say, saints live like saints.

In chapters 5–6 of Ephesians, we will learn how to be imitators of God, what is proper for saints (like us), being light in the Lord, and its bearings on our relationships. This outward display of the identity we've received is imperfect on most days; but even still, if it is the name you've been given then it is the life you can live.

Jackie

EPHESIANS 5

[1] Therefore, be imitators of God, as dearly loved children, [2] and walk in love, as Christ also loved us and gave himself for us, a sacrificial and fragrant offering to God. [3] But sexual immorality and any impurity or greed should not even be heard of among you, as is proper for saints. [4] Obscene and foolish talking or crude joking are not suitable, but rather giving thanks. [5] For know and recognize this: Every sexually immoral or impure or greedy person, who is an idolater, does not have an inheritance in the kingdom of Christ and of God.

LIGHT VERSUS DARKNESS

[6] Let no one deceive you with empty arguments, for God's wrath is coming on the disobedient because of these things. [7] Therefore, do not become their partners. [8] For you were once darkness, but now you are light in the Lord. Walk as children of light— [9] for the fruit of the light consists of all goodness, righteousness, and truth— [10] testing what is pleasing to the Lord. [11] Don't participate in the fruitless works of darkness, but instead expose them. [12] For it is shameful even to mention what is done by them in secret. [13] Everything exposed by

the light is made visible, [14] for what makes everything visible is light. Therefore it is said:

Get up, sleeper, and rise up from the dead, and Christ will shine on you.

CONSISTENCY IN THE CHRISTIAN LIFE

[15] Pay careful attention, then, to how you walk—not as unwise people but as wise— [16] making the most of the time, because the days are evil. [17] So don't be foolish, but understand what the Lord's will is. [18] And don't get drunk with wine, which leads to reckless living, but be filled by the Spirit: [19] speaking to one another in psalms, hymns, and spiritual songs, singing and making music with your heart to the Lord, [20] giving thanks always for everything to God the Father in the name of our Lord Jesus Christ, [21] submitting to one another in the fear of Christ.

WIVES AND HUSBANDS

[22] Wives, submit to your husbands as to the Lord, [23] because the husband is the head of the wife as Christ is the head of the church. He is the Savior of the body. [24] Now as the church submits to Christ, so also wives are to submit to their husbands in everything. [25] Husbands, love your wives, just as Christ loved the church and gave himself for her [26] to make her holy, cleansing her with the washing of water by the word. [27] He did this to present the church to himself in splendor, without spot or wrinkle or anything like that, but holy and blameless. [28] In the same way, husbands are to love their wives as their own bodies. He who loves his wife loves himself. [29] For no one ever hates his own flesh but provides and cares for it, just as Christ does for the church, [30] since we are members of his body. [31] For this reason a man will leave his father and mother and be joined to his wife, and the two will become one flesh. [32] This mystery is profound, but I am talking about Christ and the church. [33] To sum up, each one of you is to love his wife as himself, and the wife is to respect her husband.

2

EPHESIANS 5:1-2

Memory Verse:

Therefore, be imitators of God, as dearly loved children, and walk in love, as Christ also loved us and gave himself for us, a sacrificial and fragrant offering to God.

Ephesians 5:1-2

IMITATORS OF GOD

By this point, the Christians in Ephesus have learned about all that's been made available to them in Christ (chapters 1–2), the unity of the church (chapters 2–3), and the right response to these blessings (chapter 4). You'll recall that with chapter 4, Paul shifted from an emphasis on orthodoxy—right belief—to orthopraxy—right practice. However, chapter breaks can be misleading. Because of them, we might assume that with the start of chapter 5 Paul is broaching upon a new idea and leaving the previous one behind. Chapter divisions aren't the creative intention of the apostles or any other Scripture writer; in fact, they are new additions to the Scriptures that serve us in many ways and potentially hinder us in others.[1]

With that in mind, read Ephesians 4 and 5, without paying attention to the chapter divisions.

1. **How does Ephesians 5:1-2 build upon chapter 4?**

2. **Explain how Paul's description of the "new self" in chapter 4 corresponds to Ephesians 5:1.**

Here we see another of Paul's contrasts threaded throughout his letter to the Ephesians. Those who are called saints (1:1)—who are heirs to the spiritual blessings of Christ described in chapter 1 and who have put on the new self "created according to God's likeness" (4:24)—are also called to "be imitators of God" (5:1). In Ephesians 4:17, Paul says, "You must no longer walk as the Gentiles do" (ESV, emphasis added). And how did the Gentiles walk exactly? In the "futility of their minds." They were "callous" and gave themselves up to "sensuality" and "every kind of impurity" (4:19, ESV). At any point that these saints practiced the Gentile way, they would fail to imitate God.

3. **Read Genesis 3:1-7.** **Using Scripture, explain how Eve's pursuit of the likeness of God is different from Paul's instruction to imitate God.**

4. **Think about some of the sinful practices you've observed in your family of origin, friend groups, and wider cultural context. In what ways do you tend to sinfully imitate them instead of God? (This is intended to be an exercise of introspection and confession, not an avenue of shame.)**

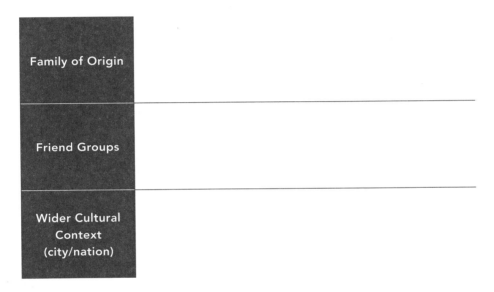

Paul will detail some specifics of what imitating God looks like in the following verses, but the heart of it is captured in verse 2: "Walk in love, as Christ also loved us and gave himself for us, a sacrificial and fragrant offering to God." Imitating the world puts self first. Power first. Pleasure first. Imitating God puts Him first. Sacrifice first. Others first. We see this in Eve's pursuit of the likeness of God in Genesis 3, which was birthed out of personal desire for the purpose of personal gain. Paul calls the saints to a pursuit of God birthed out of Christ's love for us and for the purpose of loving others.

5. Read over Ephesians 1:3-6; Romans 8:12-14; and Jude 1:20-22. Consider Paul's words to "imitate God as dearly loved children." What is the relationship between being a child of God and being an imitator of God? In other words, how should "adoptive sonship" influence the way we live?

You'll recall from early in our study that Melissa described how our identity as adopted children of God comes with the privileges of "name (saint), estate (in Christ), and inheritance (eternal life with Christ)." As saints we're called in all things to imitate God in the example of Christ Jesus and the power of the Spirit.

6. Write out the following texts in the space provided. Then circle each mention of love you see.

◆ Ephesians 1:4-6

◆ Ephesians 2:4-7

◆ Ephesians 5:25-27

7. Explain how the descriptions of the way the Father loves you and Christ loves the church in question 6 might clarify what Paul means by "walk in love."

Love is defined broadly in our society. For some, it is primarily sentimental. For others, it guarantees freedom of expression. But for Paul, neither definition is in view. To walk in love, as Christ loved us, is to live toward God and others as Christ does.

8. Read Galatians 2:20 and Hebrews 10:5-14. What does it mean that Christ "gave himself" or was an "offering"?

9. Now read Leviticus 1:1-9. To say that Christ's offering was fragrant is to highlight the pleasure God the Father took in the sacrifice of His Son. Reflect on the idea of God taking "pleasure" in Christ's self-giving and write down your thoughts:

10. Consider Paul's description of Christ in Colossians 1:15-18 and meditate on how *that* Christ "gave Himself" for you. What questions, praises, ideas come to mind?

11. If Paul's original point is "Be imitators of God" who "walk in love, as Christ loved us," would it be fair to assume that imitating God and walking in love must include the giving up of oneself? Explain what might have led me to that conclusion.

In his commentary on Ephesians, theologian Frank Thielman writes,

> The love of God and the love of Christ provide the models for individuals within the church to follow in their relationships with one another. The specific ethical instructions of 4:25-31 are practical examples of how the church, as God's re-created humanity, can fulfill the mandate implied in its creation in God's image (4:24) and in its status as the body of Christ. The love believers [have] for one another should imitate the richly gracious and self-sacrificing nature of God's love in Christ for them.[2]

Let your mind dwell on this today.

Reflect

What words or thoughts come to mind when you think about the phrase "as Christ loved us"? Note them here.

Bearing in mind everything you've learned today, write a 1-2 sentence description of how you're being called to live in light of today's Scripture.

How do you fare when you compare your response to that last question to how you lived today? To your parenting or your work? To your neighborliness or caretaking? To your casual friendships?

AS IS PROPER AMONG SAINTS

Read Ephesians 5.

Moving further into Ephesians 5, Paul's instructions continue with some admonitions against behaviors that are opposed to our identity as "saints" and "children of light." The warnings in these passages could come across as unnecessary to some. If we are "saints," why should we be warned about things like judgment and the like? As we will soon learn, God uses the warnings of Scripture to preserve us. With our new identity, there comes an expectation that we will be who we are in Christ, living as Jesus did, and displaying in our lives and even in our speech, the holiness that befits our new nature.

12. **Read Ephesians 5:3-6. What does Paul mean by "saint?" (Recall what you learned in Ephesians 1.) How does that inform what he might mean by "as is proper among saints" and "which are out of place" (5:3-4, ESV)?**

13. **Compare the culture of the Gentiles described in Ephesians 4:17-19 with the culture of the new self described in Ephesians 4:20-24. What are the differences? What further insight does this give you into that which "is proper among saints"?**

In my own ministry, I've made a practice of referring to saints as saints. Articulating this in whatever forum God allows serves to remind men and women of who they are so as to encourage them in how to live. There is an expectation that comes with being new. Having a new self must result in having a new way of being. Paul helps us see that our new way of being includes the way we use our entire body—the mind, the mouth, the words, and everything else.

EPHESIANS 5:3-6

Memory Verse:

Therefore, be imitators of God, as dearly loved children, and walk in love, as Christ also loved us and gave himself for us, a sacrificial and fragrant offering to God.

Ephesians 5:1-2

Read James 3:6-12, paying special attention to verses 11-12. James is basically saying that the nature of a thing should correspond with whatever it produces—a fig tree will never yield olives, only figs.

14. **Using James 3:6-12 and Ephesians 5:4, explain the connection between saints and their speech.**

15. **I find it interesting that Paul doesn't simply restrict the content of the saint's speech by saying "don't talk this way" and nothing more. He offers an alternative form of speech, which is _____ .**

16. Read Romans 1:21 and Colossians 2:6-7. **What do these verses teach you about thankfulness (Eph. 5:4)?**

Thankfulness is just as much of an outworking of the new self as sexual purity is. This is because thankfulness is God-oriented speech. Paul's word to the Ephesians (and to us) is about much more than simply changing the way we talk as saints; it's about a total reorienting of our language around the glory of God.

17. **Identify a moment this week when you used your words to imitate someone or something other than God. If the same scenario happened tomorrow, describe what it would look like to "let there be thanksgiving" instead (ESV).**

18. Now read Galatians 5:19-21 and 1 Corinthians 6:9-10, **then compare those texts to Ephesians 5:5. What do you notice?**

19. **Why might Paul need to remind saints of these things?**

20. Read Exodus 34:6-7; Romans 1:21; and Ephesians 2:1-3. **What is God's wrath a response to?**

As an incentive, Paul makes it clear that the person who practices sexual immorality, impurity, and covetousness will not inherit the kingdom of Christ and God. It may seem odd that such a severe point would be made to "saints," but as we all know, it is fairly easy for us to forget and/or presume upon God's grace. The reminder of God's wrath trains us not to take holiness lightly.

Moses reminded God's people of the judgment that would come if they continued in disobedience (see also Deut. 7), and we see Paul doing much the same. This isn't to say that occasionally disobeying God in these ways warrants an eternal penalty. Paul has already made the case that these saints are forgiven, redeemed, and secured in Ephesians 1. However, if and when these sexual sins and covetousness rule the life of an individual in the church, it is evidence that person is not in fact a saint and therefore excluded from the inheritance saints will receive.

> For people who do evil to inherit God's Lordship is self-contradiction. Hence it entails a tacit invitation to change. In principle the old practices lie behind them, belonging to their past. They must (logical must) remove these anomalies to prove the authenticity of their calling as holy people who belong to God (1:2–3).[3]

Any teaching that would tempt the Ephesian saints to believe that continuing in unrepentant sin won't lead to judgment is considered "empty" (Eph. 5:6). Let's look at a few Bible translations to get a sense of the meaning here.

Let no man deceive you with vain words:
for because of these things cometh the wrath
of God upon the children of disobedience.

Let no one deceive you with empty words,
for because of these things the wrath of
God comes upon the sons of disobedience.

Let no one deceive you with empty arguments,
for God's wrath is coming on the
disobedient because of these things.

21. Now read the following texts:

Be careful that no one takes you captive through philosophy
and empty deceit based on human tradition, based
on the elements of the world, rather than Christ.

COLOSSIANS 2:8

Don't turn away to follow worthless things that
can't profit or rescue you; they are worthless.

1 SAMUEL 12:21

Considering both texts and the above translations of Ephesians 5:6, what do you conclude Paul means by "empty words"?

22. Read 2 Peter 2:1-3,18-19; 2 Peter 3:3-4; and Jude 4. What particular false teaching regarding God's wrath has always threatened the church? What is its relationship with sexual practices?

From as far back as the garden, the authority or lordship of God has been called into question. With Ephesians 5:6, Paul reminds his readers that the grace and love of God is not license for sin; rather, it ushers in a new level of expectation for behavior and conduct—the expectation that one's actions imitate God. To live counter to God's vision for the Christian life is an invitation for His wrath.

23. **What are some of the temptations—both personal (example: fear of man) and cultural (example: loss of social status)—to *not be sure* about the wrath of God?**

    ◆ **Personal**

    ◆ **Cultural**

24. **What's at stake if the saints believe that the sexually immoral, impure, and covetous will inherit the kingdom of God? What would it say about the holiness of God?**

Consider John Stott's words in closing:

It would be easy for Christians to speed-read a paragraph like this, without pausing for reflection, on the assumption that it applies to unbelievers, not to us. Has not Paul assured us in the earlier part of his letter of our heavenly inheritance, taught us that the Holy Spirit within us is God's guarantee, even foretaste and first installment, of it 'until we acquire possession of it', and prayed that our eyes might be opened to see 'the riches of the glory of the inheritance' which will one day be ours? Yes, indeed he has. At the same time he also addresses to us this warning about the danger of forfeiting our inheritance in God's kingdom. How can we reconcile these things? Only by recalling that assurance of salvation is neither a synonym nor an excuse for presumption. And if we should fall into a life of greedy immorality, we would be supplying clear evidence that we are after all idolaters, not worshipers of God, disobedient people instead of obedient, and so the heirs not of heaven but of hell. The apostle gives us a solemn warning; we shall be wise to heed it.[4]

Reflect

Apply Paul's teaching in Ephesians 5:3-6 to your own life. Confess your patterns and tendencies toward immorality. Confess the parts of your life that imitate the Gentiles. And praise God for your identity as a saint. Ask Him to help you live fully as who you are in Him today.

YOU ARE LIGHT

Read Ephesians 5 from a translation other than the one you've been reading.

Darkness and light are popular metaphors in the Scriptures. Darkness is usually representative of evil or some form of ignorance. Light most commonly symbolizes moral purity, truth, and righteousness. In Ephesians 5, Paul explains that "in the Lord," Christians are considered "light." What a glorious description.

Read Ephesians 5:7-14.

Paul doesn't simply say that at one time the Ephesians walked in darkness. Remember the chart you filled in last week (p.128)? He says, "For you were once darkness."

25. **Think about your life before becoming a saint and follow these prompts as a way to remember what it meant for you to be darkness.**

    ◆ **In darkness, how did I talk and what did I talk about?**

    ◆ **In darkness, how did I think and what did I think about?**

    ◆ **In darkness, how did I love and what did I love?**

    ◆ **In darkness, how did I dishonor my body?**

If these are hard for you to answer because you've been a saint for so long, consider some of your strongest temptations to sin in each of those categories and you'll see the callbacks to who you were in darkness.

Memory Verse:

Therefore, be imitators of God, as dearly loved children, and walk in love, as Christ also loved us and gave himself for us, a sacrificial and fragrant offering to God.

Ephesians 5:1-2

Paul reminds the Ephesians of who they used to be by reiterating who they are—"but now you are *light* in the Lord" (emphasis added).

26. **Think about your life after becoming a saint and follow these prompts as a way to see what it means for you to be light in the Lord.**

   ◆ As light in the Lord, how do I talk and what do I talk about?

   ◆ As light in the Lord, how do I think and what do I think about?

   ◆ As light in the Lord, how do I love and what do I love?

   ◆ As light in the Lord, how do I honor my body?

Here we have another incentive for why we should avoid being sexually immoral and covetous (5:3). Simply put, it's not who we are. What happened that you, who were darkness, are now light in the Lord?

Ephesians 2 happened:

> *And you were dead in the trespasses and sins in which you once walked . . . But God, being rich in mercy, because of the great love with which he loved us, even when we were dead in our trespasses, made us alive together with Christ.* **EPHESIANS 2:1-4 ,ESV**

And Ephesians 5 happened:

> *Awake, O sleeper, and arise from the dead, and Christ will shine on you.* **EPHESIANS 5:14, ESV**

Self-denial comes second to conversion. So if we are "children of light" (5:8) who have been delivered into Christ's "marvelous light" (1 Pet. 2:9)—if darkness is neither who we are or what defines our existence—then the natural response is to live like it.

With verse 9 Paul adds a note of clarification to his point. Consider:

> Paul now inserts a parenthetical comment expanding on the idea that 'children of the light' should 'walk' in a way appropriate to the basic orientation of their existence. Just as children share their parent's nature, so the fruit of a plant shares the nature of the plant that produced it. If Paul's readers are light and are children of the light, then they should produce "fruit" appropriate to the light.[5]

27. **What is the fruit of light?**

28. **Using Scripture, define *goodness*, *righteousness*, and *truth*.**

GOODNESS	
RIGHTEOUSNESS	
TRUTH	

Though clear in their meaning, goodness, righteousness, and truth may be unclear in their application. There are decisions to be made, conversations to have, jobs to apply for, prayers to pray, churches to join and churches to leave and in any given scenario, we can know what to do while not actually knowing what to do. Hence Paul's charge for us to "discern what is pleasing" (Eph. 5:10, ESV). Failure to be discerning, as children of light, can lead us right back into darkness if we're not wise.

29. **Write down every verse number in 5:10-17 that speaks to the concept of discernment/wisdom.**

In her book *All That's Good*, Hannah Anderson writes these words that are helpful for us:

> *Broadly speaking, discernment is the ability to sort between a host of options and pick what is good. It carries the idea of judging the merits of something, being able to distinguish between good and bad and what is best . . . In other words, discernment does not change the challenges we face; it changes our ability to face them.*[6]

30. **Read Proverbs 2; James 1:5; and James 3:13-17. Wisdom is often framed as being primarily intellectual or philosophical in nature. After reading the texts above, how does wisdom influence ethics, our faith in practice?**

31. **Describe a time when discerning what was pleasing to the Lord helped you walk as a child of light.**

Apart from the power of God at work in us through His Spirit, we have no hope of "discern[ing] what is pleasing to the Lord." Because of the indwelling Spirit, though, this way of living is possible. Elsewhere Paul refers to this as having "the mind of Christ" (1 Cor. 2:16), and it is from this place that our thoughts overflow into actions and living. In other words, godly discernment leads to walking in love and light.

Earlier in this chapter, Paul provided us with five motivations for why we should "walk as children of light." Here again, in verse 11, he repeats the same thing in a different way: "Don't participate in the fruitless works of darkness."

32. Using what you've learned thus far, explain each motivation for why we should not "participate in the fruitless works of darkness."

◆ Ephesians 5:3

◆ Ephesians 5:5

◆ Ephesians 5:6

◆ Ephesians 5:8

Paul tells the saints to avoid the dark and sinful ways of others, but instead, expose them.

33. Read John 3:19-21. What are the "works of darkness" we are to expose?

Someone might assume that exposing darkness is a primarily verbal act. What's interesting is that in the next verse (5:12), Paul says: "For it is shameful even to speak of the things that they do in secret." It can seem as if Paul is suggesting a way to expose darkness that doesn't focus on speech at all, since it is "shameful" to even "speak of the things they do." It is also possible that Paul isn't putting a restriction on the means of exposing darkness (verbal) but on the method. As if to say, "If it is shameful to even speak of the things they do, there should be a level of modesty and dignity in the way you choose to speak about it."

34. Using Ephesians, how do you think Paul expects us to practically "expose them"?

35. Read 2 Timothy 2:23-26; Proverbs 15:4; and 1 Peter 3:14-17. How does the speech of a "child of light" expose darkness?

36. Now read Matthew 5:13-16 and Philippians 2:14-15. How does the life of a "child of light" expose darkness?

In Ephesians 5:14, Paul says, "Awake, O sleeper, and arise from the dead, and Christ will shine on you" (ESV). It's possible that this is an allusion to Isaiah 60:1—"Arise, shine, for your light has come, and the glory of the Lord has risen upon you" (ESV). But it can also be considered an example of how to expose darkness as a child of light. As John Calvin puts it: "He (Paul) therefore represents Christ as uttering a voice which is constantly heard in the preaching of the gospel."[7] We don't speak as dead people to dead people. We speak as children of light as we point to Christ, the Son who will shine on all who will look towards Him in faith!

Reflect ────────────────────────────

You may have a circumstance now where you want to do what is good, right, and true but you don't know what that actually looks like. Take some time to write down a prayer for the wisdom to understand what the will of the Lord is.

RELATIONSHIPS IN THE LORD

Read or listen to Ephesians 5.

It's easy to get stuck in the weeds with texts like Ephesians 5:22-33. They exist as a topic of many debates, conferences, curricula, books, and dinner conversations. A common mistake in the banter around headship and submission is how often those instructions get lifted out of the overall context of Ephesians. So much so that if one were to ask—"How does a wife's submission to her husband in Ephesians 5 correspond with Christ unifying the church into one new man in Ephesians 3–4?"—many of us would be left with nothing to say. So instead of dwelling on the trees, let's spend some time examining the forest that contains them.

37. **Read Ephesians 1:7-10 by means of review. What does Paul say is the "mystery of God's will," and what does it have to do with the concept of unity?**

Memory Verse:

Therefore, be imitators of God, as dearly loved children, and walk in love, as Christ also loved us and gave himself for us, a sacrificial and fragrant offering to God.

Ephesians 5:1-2

An integral part of God's plan is the unifying of peoples and groups under the headship of Christ. The word *unity*, as one commentator points out, is a word that "was used of gathering things together and presenting them as a whole."[8] One of the clear messages of Ephesians is this idea that in Christ, diversity and distinction aren't hindrances to unity. Sin is. And the good news is, sin is defeated. Every wall has been torn down so all that's left is peace.

38. **Fill in the blanks. Christ is bringing together:**

Ephesians 1:10 _____ and _____

Ephesians 2:1-10 _____ and _____

Ephesians 2:11-22 _____ and _____

In consideration of Paul's emphasis on unity, we must question what the source of all this disunity is and how it shows up in our relationships with one another. One of the most necessary and potentially contentious ones being the relationship between husband and wife.

39. **Read Genesis 3, paying special attention to verses 12,15, and 16. What is the source of all relational dysfunction? How did it show up in our first parents' relationship with one another?**

The differences between men and women in their bodies, minds, hormones, and so on were intended for holy collaboration in taking dominion of the earth. But as sin always does, these differences became a means for dysfunction.

> *Our bodies themselves teach us that we are meant to work cooperatively for the good of each other and the broader community. In fact, the very differences between us are given to enable us to steward the earth, "to be fruitful and multiply" in both a literal and an archetypal sense. It's not surprising then, that when pride enters the picture, the very thing designed to unite us turns into a source of division and competition.*[9]

The present disunity between men and women, husbands and wives, is at play when texts such as Ephesians 5:22-33 are used to draw a line in the sand between us rather than explored in light of the cosmic unity Christ is moving us towards. The "household codes" as they're commonly called (see p.167 for more), move all the orthodoxy and orthopraxy Paul laid out in chapters 1–5 from the brain and into the body. They are to be actively lived out in daily life.

40. **In Ephesians 5:22, who is directly addressed and how might this establish Paul's understanding of the equality of both sexes?**

41. **Read Genesis 1:27 along with Galatians 3:28 and explain how both texts affirm the value of women.**

42. **If someone were to suggest that women should submit to all men universally, how would you use Ephesians 5:22 as an argument against it?**

Ephesians 5 began with the calls to imitate God and walk in love, and Paul does not deviate from that instruction with 5:22-24. For Paul, this instruction about submission is rooted fully in the example of Jesus. "Paul pictures the wife's submission as the recognition of the authority of a husband who imitates the self-sacrificial, nurturing, and supporting roles that Christ fills with respect to the church."[10] When a marriage is functioning as designed by the Lord, both the husband's leadership and the wife's submission are ways in which we imitate Christ.

43. Read Romans 8:7 and 10:3. **All people are to submit to:**

Read Romans 13:1,5 and Titus 3:1. **Believers are to submit to:**

Read Ephesians 5:21 and 1 Corinthians 16:16. **Believers are to submit to:**

Read Colossians 3:18 and Titus 2:3-5. **Wives are to submit to:**

One only need to read an article or listen to a few sermons involving the word *submission* to learn how broadly the word is applied, in both positive and negative forms—sometimes to the detriment of a woman's dignity and even safety.

44. Below I've given you a list of what submission is and isn't using Ephesians 5. Respond to each statement with an explanation from Ephesians and/or other Scriptures.

SUBMISSION IS CHRIST FOCUSED.
Response:

SUBMISSION IS NOT THE SAME THING AS SUBJECTION.
Response:

SUBMISSION DOESN'T IMPLY FEMALE INFERIORITY.
Response:

SUBMISSION IS VOLUNTARY.
Response:

SUBMISSION IS ACTIVE.
Response:

45. If a husband is to love his wife as Christ would, which would imply loving leadership that is wise, holy, and safe, how should "wives should submit in everything to their husbands" (5:24, ESV) be understood?

The distinct call for wives to submit doesn't undermine Paul's overall emphasis on unity, that is unless we let it. **Review Ephesians 4:1-16** and consider how the church is one body, with many members, different gifts, and yet, "when each part is working properly" our differences are in service to our oneness.

46. How does Ephesians 4:1-16 inform the call to submission in Ephesians 5?

Consider these words from biblical scholar Lynn Cohick:

> The unity of Christ's body is made manifest in the oneness of Jew and
> Gentile. Here the view has shifted slightly, with the emphasis on the
> unity reflected in the oneness of husband and wife. The key note of
> unity which has sounded throughout the epistle rises in volume with
> the marriage metaphor. Even more, Paul reshapes the body metaphor
> of husband/wife so that it covers the entire body of Christ. Thus the
> theme of unity and the body/flesh metaphors serve three related images:
> husband and wife as one flesh, individual believers united in one body,
> and Christ united with the church, his body. [11]

47. What is the reason Paul supplies for why wives are to submit to husbands?

*For the husband is the _____ of the wife even as
Christ is the _____ of the church, his body, and is
himself its _____. EPHESIANS 5:23, ESV*

48. A husband as head of the wife is compared to Christ as head of the church. If headship were purely authoritarian in nature, Paul could've continued the metaphor by calling attention to Christ's lordship of the church. The direction he takes instead is to bring attention to Christ as "Savior" of the church. Why do you think that is? Use 5:25-30 to explain.

Headship isn't without the connotation of authority but this authority is qualified by Paul in his description of Christ. Christ loved the church by giving Himself up for the church, a reference back to Ephesians 5:2. This self giving on the part of Christ was for a purpose—to cleanse, sanctify, and present the church to Himself as holy. In the same way, the husband as head is a position of leadership, yes, but leadership that is loving, nourishing, self giving, and godly in its application.

49. Read Ephesians 5:25-33 (pp.142-143). (Circle) every time you see a reference to *love*.

50. When we think about the common understanding of "headship," how should Paul's emphasis on the husband's call to "love" redefine our own view of a husband as the "head"?

The kingdom of God transforms headship in direct opposition to the way it would be expected in a society that supremely values power, honor, and status. According to Paul, headship manifests itself through sacrifice and love, rather than having the head preserve its own life and receive love in a self-focused and self-benefiting manner. Ironically, this reversal of expectations is precisely what leads to the fulfillment of the one flesh union of Genesis, for both the husband and the wife, and Christ and the church. Headship, thus, is centered on, not just qualified by, the defining event of the crucifixion. As Christ brings greater unity to the body, Paul likewise calls the husband to fulfill the one flesh union through love and sacrifice.[12]

Reflect

If you are married, pray for God's grace to be the wife that honors His vision for marriage. Pray the same for your husband.

If you are single, pray for God to give you wisdom and insight to help you use what you've learned to encourage other women.

HOUSEHOLD CODES

Paul's instruction for submission in Ephesians 5:21–6:9 is one of
three New Testament passages of Scripture (along with Colossians 3:18–
4:1 and 1 Peter 2:18–3:7) that have come to be known as household codes.

"In the New Testament, many derivatives of *oikos* (literally, 'house') are used to refer to the members and affairs of a household. Consequently, the terms 'house' and 'household' are often used interchangeably in translation. The term may delineate an immediate family, as well as those employed in the service of that family (Matt. 13:57; 24:45; John 4:53; Acts 16:31). Descendants of a particular nation may also be described as a house or household as in Matthew 10:6 and Luke 1:27, 69. 'Household' or 'house,' moreover, may point to the property or the management of the affairs and belongings of a family or clan (Acts 7:10).

"Next to the state, the household was the most important unit in the Greco-Roman world, largely because of its role as a guarantor of stability in society. If order prevailed in the household, so it would in the state. Just as the household was basic to society, so it was to Christianity. The life of the early church centered in houses or households (e.g. Acts 2:2, 46; 12:12; Rom. 16:5, 23; 1 Cor. 16:19). Household groups were the basic units that made up the church in any given locale.

"Not only was the church composed of household groups, the household itself was often the focus of the church's evangelistic activity. Several texts mention the conversion of entire households: Acts 11:14; 16:15, 31–34; 18:8. In the world in which the early church emerged, the household was organized around the head, and solidarity was expressed in a common religion. So it was that the faith of the head of the household was the faith of the entire household. Whenever the head of a household was converted and baptized, the remainder of his house usually followed suit as an expression of loyalty and religious unity. The motivation for conversion was at times social and not wholly individual, though in baptism each confessed Christ as Lord and showed forth His death and resurrection.

"Household ideals also impacted the early church in significant ways. Household terms were used by the New Testament writers to express theological ideas. The church was referred to as the 'household' of faith or of God (Gal. 6:10; Eph. 2:19). Household roles were appropriated by the Christian community: Christians were 'servants' of God, and their leaders were 'stewards' (1 Cor. 4:1; Titus 1:7; 1 Pet. 4:10). Because the household was so central to ancient society, much attention was given to delineating and clarifying the roles of the members of a household, be they family or servant. Standardized rules for behavior or domestic codes were developed in society, and these were adapted for use in the early church. Examples of lists of house rules or codes may be found in Colossians 3:18–4:1; Ephesians 5:21–6:9; 1 Peter 2:13–3:7. The church reinterpreted these rules in the light of their faith so as to assert their distinctiveness in the larger world."[13]

Excerpted from the Holman Bible Dictionary.

DAY FIVE

5

EPHESIANS 5

Memory Verse:

Therefore, be

imitators of God, as

dearly loved children,

and walk in love, as

Christ also loved

us and gave himself

for us, a sacrificial

and fragrant

offering to God.

Ephesians 5:1-2

WRAP UP

Read or listen to Ephesians 5 one final time.

Paul has taught us much this week about how saints are to live, all of it rooted in the call from Ephesians 5:1-2 to "be imitators of God" who "walk in love." But like we've said many times, the instructions in this chapter are not to be divorced from the rest of the letter.

Today, I want you to reflect on what you've learned in Ephesians 1–5, continuing the work of drawing connections between theology and practice Paul brings together in this book.

51. Reflect on what Ephesians 5 reveals about:

God the Father	God the Son	God the Spirit

52. In your copy of the text on pages 142-143, circle any abundance language you see. Look for words like *all*, *everything*, and *always*.

53. Ephesians 5 contains three contrasting pairs, which are listed below. Next to each one, summarize the main point Paul wants readers to understand from that contrasting set of images. Look back through your notes from this week of study to aid in your summary.

◆ Saints vs. idolaters

◆ Light vs. darkness

◆ Wise vs. unwise

54. Pick one text from Ephesians 1–2 that feels like an anchor passage for Paul's instructions to husbands and wives in Ephesians 5:22-33. Write that passage in the space below.

55. Review Ephesians 5:19-21. We'll always have room for growth when it comes to living in the fullness of our identity as saints. How do you sense the Spirit convicting you to live differently in light of the commands in these verses?

Spend a few minutes in prayer. Confess the ways you've failed to imitate God lately. Praise Him for the abundant love, grace, and peace that is yours in Christ.

WATCH

Watch the Session Six video and take notes below.

TO ACCESS THE VIDEO SESSIONS, USE THE INSTRUCTIONS
IN THE BACK OF YOUR BIBLE STUDY BOOK.

DISCUSS

Discuss the following questions with your Bible study group. A more extensive leader guide is available for free download at **lifeway.com/ephesiansstudy.**

1. Which day of personal study had the most impact on you, and why? What lingering questions do you have?

2. How did what you heard on the video clarify, reinforce, or give new insight to what you studied this session?

3. Based on your personal study and the video conversation, discuss what it means to imitate God—and what it *doesn't* mean.

4. How has your understanding of Paul's instructions to wives and husbands shifted or grown now that you've studied it with the full letter in view?

5. How do you want to live differently in the week to come because of what we've studied this week?

EPHESIANS 6

EMPOWERED
& EQUIPPED

The closing segments of Paul's letter feel a bit like channel surfing. The remote clicks and we end up on a show with two parents and a child working through their intergenerational issues. On another is a documentary summarizing the economic motivations and sinful advantages of the slave trade. Turn the channel again and it's a demon tormenting through entertainment. Children and parents, slaves and masters, devils and demons and then . . . Tychicus.

Paul's diversity of subjects is intentional. He is still drawing out the implications of the previous chapters by communicating their place in the familial, social, and spiritual life of Christians. Then as he often does, he ends it all with the mention of a name not often quoted by us but eternally remembered in God's kingdom.

Jackie

EPHESIANS 6

CHILDREN AND PARENTS

Children, obey your parents in the Lord, because this is right. ² Honor your father and mother, which is the first commandment with a promise, ³ so that it may go well with you and that you may have a long life in the land. ⁴ Fathers, don't stir up anger in your children, but bring them up in the training and instruction of the Lord.

SLAVES AND MASTERS

⁵ Slaves, obey your human masters with fear and trembling, in the sincerity of your heart, as you would Christ. ⁶ Don't work only while being watched, as people-pleasers, but as slaves of Christ, doing God's will from your heart. ⁷ Serve with a good attitude, as to the Lord and not to people, ⁸ knowing that whatever good each one does, slave or free, he will receive this back from the Lord. ⁹ And masters, treat your slaves the same way, without threatening them, because you know that both their Master and yours is in heaven, and there is no favoritism with him.

CHRISTIAN WARFARE

[10] Finally, be strengthened by the Lord and by his vast strength. [11] Put on the full armor of God so that you can stand against the schemes of the devil. [12] For our struggle is not against flesh and blood, but against the rulers, against the authorities, against the cosmic powers of this darkness, against evil, spiritual forces in the heavens. [13] For this reason take up the full armor of God, so that you may be able to resist in the evil day, and having prepared everything, to take your stand. [14] Stand, therefore, with truth like a belt around your waist, righteousness like armor on your chest, [15] and your feet sandaled with readiness for the gospel of peace. [16] In every situation take up the shield of faith with which you can extinguish all the flaming arrows of the evil one. [17] Take the helmet of salvation and the sword of the Spirit—which is the word of God. [18] Pray at all times in the Spirit with every prayer and request, and stay alert with all perseverance and intercession for all the saints. [19] Pray also for me, that the message may be given to me when I open my mouth to make known with boldness the mystery of the gospel. [20] For this I am an ambassador in chains. Pray that I might be bold enough to speak about it as I should.

PAUL'S FAREWELL

[21] Tychicus, our dearly loved brother and faithful servant in the Lord, will tell you all the news about me so that you may be informed. [22] I am sending him to you for this very reason, to let you know how we are and to encourage your hearts.

[23] Peace to the brothers and sisters, and love with faith, from God the Father and the Lord Jesus Christ. [24] Grace be with all who have undying love for our Lord Jesus Christ.

DAY ONE
1

EPHESIANS 6:1-4

Memory Verse:

Finally, be strengthened by the Lord and by his vast strength. Put on the full armor of God so that you can stand against the schemes of the devil.

Ephesians 6:10-11

CHILDREN & PARENTS

Read through Ephesians 6

Venturing into Ephesians 6, we continue learning how to apply the spiritual realities of our life with Christ to our day-to-day lives—whether it be in our marriages, our parenting, or within oppressive systems in society. Calling attention to the relationship between believing parents and children shows how comprehensive God intends for our imitation of His nature to be. There is no place in the believer's life that is off limits to the glory of God.

Now reread Ephesians 6:1-4.

Different from wives who are called to submit, and husbands who are called to love, Paul tells children to obey. There are three motivations added that we will work through. Children are to obey their parents in the Lord because it is 1) right, 2) law, and 3) life.

IT IS RIGHT (v. 1)

The term *right* refers to behavior that would be considered "proper" or "reasonable." Though a child's obedience to parents should be seen as a virtue, it isn't always viewed as such, especially from the perspective of children who aren't yet "in the Lord."

1. Read Romans 1:28-32 and 2 Timothy 3:1-2. **Considering the context of Romans 1 and 2 Timothy 3, how should we think about children's obedience to parents?**

Since Paul is addressing children who are "in the Lord," he intends to give instructions for how they too are to "walk in a manner worthy of the calling to which [they] have been called" (Eph. 4:1).

2. **Read Luke 2:41-51. What is the relationship between Christ's obedience to His Father in heaven and His continual obedience to His earthly parents?**

Christ, the Son of God, was first and foremost obedient to God His Father (Phil. 2:5-7), and out of the overflow of that love flowed obedience toward Mary and Joseph. This affirms for us Paul's mention of children obeying "in the Lord." Please note, it is not as though the instruction shouldn't apply to all children because it does. However, the expectation of children who have been incorporated into Christ's family is that they will live altogether differently than unbelieving children.

3. **You may be in proximity to children who don't seem to display any evidence of being "in the Lord." Imagine you were sitting down with them and decided to instruct them on how they can be "in the Lord" as you are. Using Ephesians 2:1-10, write a paragraph to teach them how they can become children of God.**

Take a moment to pray for the children in your life. Whether it be your own children, students, nephews, nieces, siblings, neighbors, and so on. Pray that those who are not yet in the Lord would be "made alive" (Eph. 2:5), and that those who are in the Lord would be "imitators of God" as "dearly loved children."

IT IS LAW (v. 2)

The second motivation Paul gives for a child's obedience to parents is the reminder that it is law.

4. What Old Testament text is Paul referencing in Ephesians 6:2?

5. What do you make of the placement of "Honor your father and your mother" in the Ten Commandments (see Ex. 20:12)? Pay attention to who's centered in the preceding commands and who's involved in the commands that follow it.

The command to honor one's parents that Paul has in view is the Fifth Commandment, found in Exodus 20:12. By restating it here, Paul connects this Mosaic law with life in Christ. As theologian Eugene Carpenter notes,

> To relate to God appropriately, people must relate properly to their fellow human being in his image...The first word directing relationships toward others focuses on parents, who stand as human partners with God in the 'creation' and nurture of persons. They are to be treated in a way that honors them for their position and their character.[1]

IT IS LIFE (v. 3)

The third and final motivation for a child's obedience is that it is life— "so that . . . you may have a long life in the land."

6. Paul's reference to Old Testament law isn't arbitrary. He draws attention to the promise attached to that specific law. Read Exodus 20:12. What is that promise?

7. Read Proverbs 15:5; Proverbs 20:20; and Proverbs 30:17. In what ways do these texts draw out the wise instruction of Ephesians 6:2?

It is debatable what Paul's use of Exodus 20:12 may mean in regards to the extended nature of an obedient child's life. There are some interpretive wrestles around if the promise "that you may live long in the land" is to be taken literally (living long) or spiritually (eternal life).[2] Though commentators land in different directions, the wise principle to be drawn out is clear: A child's obedience to his/her parents in the Lord increases the probability of having a life that is shaped by wisdom, fruitfulness, and potential longevity.

8. **Now read Ephesians 6:4 again. Read the following commentary excerpt alongside it.**

    A Roman father had absolute power over his family. He could sell them as slaves, he could make them work in his fields even in chains, he could take the law into his own hands, for the law was in his own hands, and punish as he liked, he could even inflict the death penalty on his child.[3]

    In what way is Paul limiting a father's abuse of authority with verse 4?

With verse 4, Paul redirects his instructions now to fathers. It is likely that both parents are in mind in his instructions regarding nourishment (v. 3) and discipline (v. 4). It is not as though mothers are relegated to the sidelines in the parenting of their children. Paul's focus on fathers is owing to their position in the family unit. Just as the headship of the husband and the authoritative elements it suggests are restrained by Paul's emphasis on "love," so too the parental authority of the father is restrained by Paul's instruction not to "provoke your children to anger."

9. **What Scriptures from Ephesians (feel free to use other passages too) should influence how believing parents parent? Explain your examples.**
    Example: "Be kind to one another, tenderhearted, forgiving one another, as God in Christ forgave you" (Eph. 4:32). *A believing parent's authority should be wielded in ways that are kind and tenderhearted, and when children sin against a parent, they should forgive, just as Christ forgave them.*

    ◆ _____

    ◆ _____

    ◆ _____

Again, here we see Paul building on everything that has come prior to this point in his letter to the Ephesians. Both the call to obey one's parents and to parent in the instruction of the Lord are examples of faith in practice, the new way of life in which saints are called to walk.

10. **Read both texts below.**

    Fathers, do not provoke your children to anger, but <u>bring them up</u> in the discipline and instruction of the Lord. EPHESIANS 6:4, ESV

    For no one ever hated his own flesh, but <u>nourishes and cherishes it</u>, just as Christ does the church. EPHESIANS 5:29, ESV

    The underlined words are the same phrase in the original Greek language. What can we conclude "bring them up" means?

    In contrast to provoking their children, fathers are to nurture their children in what?

Discipline may have punitive aspects but more than that, Paul intends for godly discipline to have educational value.

11. **Look up and read Hebrews 12:5-11 and 2 Timothy 3:16-17. How do these texts inform your view of "bring them up in the discipline and instruction of the Lord" (ESV)?**

In addition to basic instruction regarding how to be a responsible human being who's potty trained and able to walk, talk, cook, count, or wash dishes, for Paul there's a greater emphasis on parental discipline and instruction being "of the Lord."

12. **Read Ephesians 4:20-21 and Deuteronomy 11:18-21. Using the verses above, what is the content, consistency, and character of a parent's godly instruction?**

Above all else, the greatest responsibility of the Christian parent is discipleship, being the person from whom your child hears about Jesus and sees the life of a saint in action. Imitating God and walking in love matters in your home as much as it does in the world.

This responsibility stretches beyond the walls of the home, too. If you don't have children, you are no less responsible for discipling those in your midst. Look for them. Love on them. Find ways to be a spiritual parent to the children in your family, church, apartment complex, neighborhood, or friend groups.

Reflect ——————————————————————

How do you sense God calling you to respond to the instruction in Ephesians 6:1-4? Write out a prayer of response as you dwell on these things.

EPHESIANS 6:5-9

Memory Verse:

Finally, be strengthened by the Lord and by his vast strength. Put on the full armor of God so that you can stand against the schemes of the devil.

Ephesians 6:10-11

SLAVES AND MASTERS

Paul began this portion of his letter by addressing husbands and wives, then children and parents. Now, he directs his attention to the relationship between slaves and masters. What Paul puts forward is theological in nature with the intention of it being lived out by the persons addressed.

Dignifying the texts before us requires that we address the historic impact of the abuses of them. Particularly on the lives of African Americans. In our study of Ephesians 6:5-9, history cannot be ignored. I have in mind those who identify or are tempted at least to restrict the full counsel of God's Word in response to the abuses of it. An example of this is Howard Thurman's grandmother, who read most of the Scriptures with the exclusion of the Pauline epistles. Howard tells the story that was told to him by his grandmother regarding her time as a slave. She recounted how a "white minister" would teach the slave/master texts from Paul three to four times a year. In response, she decided on an inward protest of all Pauline literature (except 1 Cor. 13). For she said, "I promised my Maker that if I ever learned to read and if freedom ever came, I would not read that part of the Bible."[4]

I can't overstate how much I empathize with Thurman's grandmother, and therefore the task before us is to look in a couple directions: 1) History and 2) Theology.

HISTORY

13. **Look up and read the following passages:**

- ◆ 1 Peter 2:13-24
- ◆ Colossians 3:22-25
- ◆ 1 Timothy 6:1
- ◆ Ephesians 6:5-9

Is there a common theme that unifies these texts? Write down what you notice.

Slavery in the Roman Empire was different from antebellum slavery in many respects. Even so, that doesn't diminish the fact that slavery is still slavery. Read the quote below to get an idea of how slavery looked in Paul's context:

In Paul's day, slavery was not based on race or religion, but on fate, chance, or birth. Defeated armies and peoples were enslaved, those captured by pirates were held as slaves, and many slaves were born to slave mothers . . . Other slaves rowed in galley ships, worked in mines or in fields, and died in the gladiatorial games. Yet all slaves shared this in common: they were owned by another.[5]

14. **"Yet all slaves shared this in common: they were owned by another." Using Genesis 1:27-28, what's problematic about that sentence from a strictly human standpoint?**

Slavery is an effect of our sinful inheritance (Gen. 3). The blessing of dominion was and is co-opted as a means of controlling other human beings. A feature of antebellum slavery in particular is the Scriptural justifications offered to maintain this domination. Scholar Lisa Bowens noted that "the struggle to save black lives was intricately linked with the struggle over sacred scriptural interpretation."[6]

Ephesians 6:5-7, along with Colossians and Philemon, were used to "sanction laws regarding slaveocracy."[7] At the core of the misuse of these passages is the belief that one class of people is inferior to another.

15. Read Galatians 3:27-29 and Colossians 3:9-11. **How do these verses undermine the idea of inferiority and superiority based on gender, ethnicity, and social status?**

The letter of Ephesians would've been read in full to the whole believing community, including husbands and wives, parents and children, and slaves and masters. Paul has previously emphasized Christ's body as a unified whole, containing diverse parts, all under the headship of Christ (Eph. 2:11-21; 4:1-16).

16. **With that in mind, how should Paul's overall emphasis on unity within diversity and Christ's headship have informed the way both a slave and a master interpreted Ephesians 6:5-9?**

In the words of Frederick Douglass:

> What do you do when you are told by the slaveholders of America that the Bible sanctions slavery? Do you go and throw your Bible into the fire . . . do you declare that a thing is bad because it has been missed, abused, and made bad use of? . . . No! You press it to your bosom all the more closely. You read it all the more diligently; and prove from its pages that it is on the side of liberty—and not on the side of slavery.[8]

THEOLOGY

17. **Looking at Ephesians 6:5, what is Paul communicating by referring to masters as "earthly" or "human" masters?**

18. **How are slaves instructed to obey their masters (vv. 5-8)?**

- ◆ _____

- ◆ _____

- ◆ _____

- ◆ _____

- ◆ _____

Obedience "with fear and trembling" may sound concerning to some. Is Paul saying "fear and trembling" is the same as "terror," either the terror of the master or his punishments? Let's read **2 Corinthians 7:13-15** to get a sense of what Paul means.

> *For this reason we have been comforted. In addition to our own comfort, we rejoiced even more over the joy Titus had, because his spirit was refreshed by all of you. For if I have made any boast to him about you, I have not been disappointed; but as I have spoken everything to you in truth, so our boasting to Titus has also turned out to be the truth. And his affection toward you is even greater as he remembers the obedience of all of you, and how you received him with fear and trembling.*

19. The church in Corinth responded to Titus "with fear and trembling." Considering the context, what does this seem to communicate?

20. If "fear and trembling" has more to do with reverence than with terror, what is Paul telling slaves to do? Rewrite Ephesians 6:5 in your own words.

21. Slaves are instructed to obey with a "sincere heart" and without "eye service" or "people pleasing." What is the motivation Paul provides for why that degree of integrity should be pursued (v. 6)?

22. If all people, both slave and free, will one day stand before the judgment seat of Christ (2 Cor. 5:10), how should we think about the way God ultimately views earthly social distinctions?

23. **Paul instructs masters to "do the same to them."** Read Ephesians 6:5-8 and Colossians 4:1. **What might Paul mean by this?**

In John Calvin's commentary on Ephesians, he notes,

> . . . that which is just and equal, is precisely what, in this passage, he calls the same things . . . the same things; for we are all ready enough to demand what is due to ourselves; but, when our own duty comes to be performed, every one attempts to plead exemption. It is chiefly, however, among persons of authority and rank that injustice of this sort prevails.[9]

Paul levels the playing field between masters and slaves in two ways. They both exist under the authority of the same Master. And now, with the instruction to masters to "do the same things" to slaves as slaves are to do to them—that being what is "fair and just"—Paul establishes equality of treatment. In a system that depends on injustice and discrimination, the slavery of the Roman Empire, and subsequently antebellum slavery, might've collapsed sooner if Paul's instructions were fully realized.

24. **Within the Roman Empire "violence was the primary foundation of the institution."[10] Threats and violence were a means of controlling slaves. With that in mind, what should we make of Paul's instructions to masters in verse 9?**

> *"With this command, Paul has cut the thread that holds the institution together."[11]*

A question that remains unanswered around Pauline slave texts is why Paul didn't advocate for the manumission of slaves within the Roman Empire. Though there is the encouragement from Paul to slaves, "But if you can gain your freedom, avail yourself of the opportunity" (1 Cor. 7:21), the lack of an explicit condemnation of slavery in addition to the returning of Onesimus to Philemon is considered problematic by some. I'd argue that in Paul's instructions, as inspired by the God of liberty, is as one commentator put it, a vision of a "new creation sibling-based fellowship on the basis of adoption as children of God."[12]

Reflect

For some of us, texts like today can feel heavy and frustrating. Those of African American descent are reminded of their ancestral heritage and how these same texts were used to do wicked things against God's image bearers. Others of us who have endured suffering under organizational, religious, or political institutions to which we were called to submit may feel some big emotions too. We should all be reckoning with the reality that even today 49.6 million people are enslaved through human trafficking networks around the world. You cannot talk about the slavery in Paul's day and ignore the human feelings and present realities for which these texts have direct implications.

With that said I encourage you, on whatever spectrum you find yourself after working through today's session, to feel your feelings. And while you do, remember your God.

What does Ephesians say about who He is, what He's done, and what He will do?

And how might that frame your view of history and current social realities?

Sit with these thoughts in quiet before the Lord today.

3

THE ARMOR OF GOD

EPHESIANS 6:10-18

By the end of Paul's letter, he's said a whole lot. After communicating the spiritual blessings we've received in Christ, emphasizing the unity of the church, and exhorting the Ephesians on the subsequent ethical responses to Christ's work on the cross, Paul wraps it all up with the challenge to "be strong in the Lord" by taking up the armor of God.

Memory Verse:

Finally, be strengthened by the Lord and by his vast strength. Put on the full armor of God so that you can stand against the schemes of the devil.

Ephesians 6:10-11

We need strength to walk in a worthy manner and to imitate the Lord. Any woman attempting to submit to her own husband will soon realize how much help she needs in the matter. Parents with believing or non-believing children too. Instructing littles and teens in the Lord is hard. And even with the basic difficulty of practical obedience, there is the reality of spiritual opposition that attempts to keep us from loving the Lord in the way He's called us.

25. Read Ephesians 6:10-18 and Ephesians 1:16-19. Write down the section of Paul's prayer from chapter 1 that corresponds to verse 6:10.

Being told to "be strong" can sound like the words of a military leader yelling from the top of his lungs. If Paul's words are read in that tone, we'd assume what he means by it is that strength in the Christian life depends on our own ability to "be strong."

26. Read 2 Timothy 2:1; Judges 6:34; and 1 Samuel 30:6. When Paul tells us to "be strong in the Lord," what does he mean? Use these verses to assist you in your conclusion.

27. Although strength is received, it doesn't mean we aren't required to "put on" (6:11) and "take up" (6:13). What other place in Ephesians does Paul use the language of putting something on?

28. What are the reasons Paul provides for why Christians must "put on the whole armor of God"?

29. Now read Ephesians 2:2; Ephesians 4:27; John 8:44; 2 Corinthians 11:14; and 1 Peter 5:8. Using these texts, describe the nature of the devil and why Christians need God's armor to "stand against" his schemes.

30. Though Satan is defeated (Heb. 2:14), that doesn't imply that he should be underestimated. What would happen if a Christian decided not to take spiritual warfare seriously? Use Scripture and experience to explain.

Overestimating the devil and thereby giving him more attention than he deserves is a perspective to avoid, but so is underestimating him. Some saints are so resistant to the idea of spiritual warfare that they move through the Christian life as if they don't have a real and legitimately powerful enemy whose entire aim is to devour them. But as Stott warns,

> A thorough knowledge of the enemy and a healthy respect for his prowess are a necessary preliminary to victory in war. Similarly, if we underestimate our spiritual enemy, we shall see no need for God's armour, we shall go out to the battle unarmed, with no weapons but our own puny strength, and we shall be quickly and ignominiously defeated.[13]

After calling the Ephesian believers to be strong in the Lord and stand against the devil, Paul doubles down on the spiritual, inhuman nature of this fight we're in.

31. "For we do not wrestle against flesh and blood . . ." (v. 12). What does Paul mean by "flesh and blood," and how does it speak to what type of battle we are engaging in?

32. Ephesians 4:25-32; Ephesians 5; and Ephesians 6:1-9 all involve human relationships. What wisdom can a Christian gain knowing that there is a spiritual dimension to all struggles within the church and the home?

Satan is said to be strategic (4:27; 6:11). As Martyn Lloyd Jones put it, "The devil has certain routes which he follows very regularly."[14] According to Lloyd Jones, these routes are: 1) The mind; 2) the realm of experience (feelings, desires, and moods); and 3) the realm of practice (behavior).

Let's briefly examine Genesis 3 and Luke 4 to identify the strategy of Satan against Eve and Jesus so that we can develop an awareness of his potential strategies in our own lives.

33. Read Genesis 3:1-6. How did Satan attack the mind?

How did Satan attack the realm of experience?

How did Satan attack the realm of practice?

34. Read Luke 4:1-13. How did Satan attack the mind?

How did Satan attack the realm of experience?

How did Satan attack the realm of practice?

'Glorify him' says the Apostle Paul, 'with your mind and with your body: whatsoever ye do in word or deed, do all things to the glory of God.' . . . And if we fail in this matter we are not only succumbing to the wiles of the devil, we are detracting from the glory of God and of the Lord Jesus Christ.[15]

Paul tells us that our wrestle isn't a human wrestle but a fight against "the rulers, against the authorities, against the cosmic powers over this present darkness, against the spiritual forces of evil in the heavenly places" (v. 12). There are categories of evil that Paul wants us to be aware of as we engage in this spiritual battle, and these levels to supernatural evil can be intimidating and even scary for us to fathom. This is why we have to be reminded of what Scripture has declared about these beings.

35. **Fill in the blanks.**

Rulers and authorities are _____ (Col. 1:16).

Rulers and authorities are _____ (Col. 2:13-15).

Rulers and authorities have been _____ (1 Pet. 3:21-22).

Rulers and authorities are _____ (Eph. 1:20-21).

The strength needed to stand is something we receive from God Himself.

36. **Read Isaiah 59:17 and Isaiah 11:5. Using these verses, whose armor are we to put on in our wrestle against evil?**

The characteristics Paul instructs Christians to put on are defined throughout the letter to the Ephesians. Let's use the previous chapters and other biblical texts to understand the description of the armor of God.

37. **Fill in the chart on the next page.**

THE BELT OF TRUTH 	Read Ephesians 1:13 and 4:25. According to these texts, what does it look like to put on truth?
THE BREASTPLATE OF RIGHTEOUSNESS 	Read Ephesians 4:29 and 5:9. According to these texts, what does it look like to "put on the breastplate of righteousness"?
SHOES The Readiness of Gospel Peace 	Read Ephesians 2:11-22 and 4:3. According to these texts, what does it look like to put on the readiness given by the gospel of peace?
THE SHIELD OF FAITH 	Read Ephesians 1:13,19; 2:8; and 3:12. According to these texts, what does it look like to "take up the shield of faith"?
THE HELMET OF SALVATION 	Read Ephesians 1:13 and 2:5-8. According to these texts, what does it look like to "take the helmet of salvation"?
THE SWORD OF THE SPIRIT The Word of God 	Read Ephesians 1:13 and 5:26. According to these texts, what does it look like to "take . . . the sword of the Spirit"?

Though the saints wrestle against a real devil, with real power, and real tactics, God has provided them with an armor that, when worn, will position them to experience the victory that Christ has already secured. Glory to God!

Paul concludes his talk about the armor of God with the call to prayer. Prayer isn't associated with any armor, but "isn't prayer the battle cry of the Christian?"[16]

38. **How has prayer assisted you in your fight against evil?**

I leave you with these final words from Martyn Lloyd Jones:

> If after considering all this, you feel discouraged, it means that you have not understood it. I am saying that you have to realize that this is the enemy. Yes, but he has already told us, 'Be strong in the Lord, and in the power of his might. Take unto you the whole armour of God.' This is the glory of the Christian position, that though I am confronted by such an enemy I need not be afraid. 'Resist the devil, and he will flee from you.' . . . But do not allow that thought, or the misunderstanding of that thought, to make you feel that you need not be vigilant in respect of the enemy. Remember, says Paul, that you have to stand after every victory. Do not relax, do not go on holiday. There is no holiday in the spiritual realm.[17]

Reflect

What encourages you as you consider the ways God is even today outfitting you for spiritual battle?

What emotions do you feel as you think about this fight? How do you think God wants you to feel, bearing in mind everything you've learned in Ephesians?

DAY FOUR

EPHESIANS 6:21-24

Memory Verse:

Finally, be strengthened by the Lord and by his vast strength. Put on the full armor of God so that you can stand against the schemes of the devil.

Ephesians 6:10-11

GRACE BE WITH YOU

Read or listen to Ephesians 6 again.

We are prone to overlook the details in Paul's conclusions to his letters, as if they weren't just as God-breathed as what came before it. At the close of Paul's letter to the Ephesians, he ends as he began—with prayer. But before he does, he wants to provide the saints with additional information about himself, which he communicates through a name not often mentioned in the New Testament.

39. Read Ephesians 6:21-22; Colossians 4:7-8; and Ephesians 3:13. **What are the reasons for Paul sending Tychicus to Ephesus?**

There can be considerable distance between Christian leaders and those they are leading, not necessarily in terms of distance but in affection. This happens when leaders primarily instruct without offering themselves in a way that displays their care and concern for the people they're leading.

40. Read 1 Thessalonians 2:17-18 and 2 Corinthians 6:11-13 in addition to Ephesians 6:21-22. **How would you describe Paul as a leader and the care he displayed for the church?**

Theologian John Stott describes Paul this way:

It is touching to see the apostle's desire to forge stronger personal links between himself and these Asian Christians. His exposition of God's new society is no mere theological theory; for he and they are members of it themselves. So they must deepen their fellowship with one another.[18]

41. Now read Ephesians 6:21; Colossians 4:7; Acts 20:4; 2 Timothy 4:12; and Titus 3:12. **List everything you learn about Tychicus from these verses.**

Tychicus is given the task to deliver three of Paul's letters (Ephesians, Colossians, and Philemon) to their recipients. Depending on your perspective of ministry, being essentially a "mailman" may come across as a less significant form of ministry when compared to that of someone like Paul.

42. Read 1 Corinthians 1:10-13 and James 2:1-4. **How have you seen division and favoritism surrounding ministry gifts and positions play out in your church experience?**

43. **If you had to a encourage a friend who is serving in a ministry position that is similar to Tychicus, one that doesn't come with the privileges and prestige of other callings, how would you encourage them? (Use Eph. 4:1-16; Eph. 6:21-24; and 1 Cor. 12 as a reference).**

Underneath our griping for significance in particular ministry positions, favoritism, and the like is a centering of worldly values along with an inordinate concern for the praises of others. In C. S. Lewis's sermon, "The Weight of Glory," Lewis describes how our ordinary longing to be told "well done" by others will be fully realized (and is) in Christ:

> I can imagine someone saying that he dislikes my idea of heaven as a place where we are patted on the back. But proud misunderstanding is behind that dislike. In the end that Face which is the delight or the terror of the universe must be turned upon each of us either with one expression or with the other, either conferring glory inexpressible or inflicting shame that can never be cured or disguised. The promise of glory is the promise, almost incredible and only possible by the work of Christ, that some of us, that any of us who really chooses, shall actually

survive that examination, shall find approval, shall please God. To please God . . . to be a real ingredient in the divine happiness . . . to be loved by God, not merely pitied, but delighted in as an artist delights in his work or a father in a son—it seems impossible, a weight or burden of glory which our thoughts can hardly sustain. But so it is. [19]

Knowing what we do about the canon of Scripture and the place of Paul's letters in it, Tychicus was clearly used by God to further the gospel in irreplaceable ways.

44. Now read Ephesians 6:23-24, the closing words of Paul's letter. **Paul's prayer for peace hearkens back to themes he's explored earlier in the letter. Find where Paul referenced peace in chapters 1, 2, and 4. How does the way Paul defined and applied peace in Ephesians speak to the necessity of praying for it?**

45. **What have you learned about love and faith through your study of Ephesians, and how does it help you understand Paul's prayer for "love with faith" (v. 23)?**

All of this peace, love, and the faith that accompanies love comes 'from God the Father and the Lord Jesus Christ.' Although elements of the peace and love for which Paul has prayed, and all of the faith that accompanies love, are attitudes and actions of human beings, those who have and do these virtues cannot take credit for them. If God answers Paul's prayer-wish, then these qualities will be gifts of God, just like the grace and peace that Paul has wished for his readers at the beginning of the letter (1:2). [20]

46. **Paul prays for grace to be received by who?**

47. Read 1 Corinthians 16:21-22. What principle can we draw from both of Paul's statements about loving God?

Reflect

Take some time now to apply Paul's closing prayer to yourself, your family, and your community.

DAY FIVE 5

EPHESIANS 6

Memory Verse:

Finally, be strengthened by the Lord and by his vast strength. Put on the full armor of God so that you can stand against the schemes of the devil.

Ephesians 6:10-11

WRAP UP

Read or listen to Ephesians 6 one final time.

Paul left no shortage of topics for his final chapter of this letter—children and parents, slaves and masters, schemes of the devil, a call to perseverance, and more. If it wasn't clear yet it should be now: Your identity as a saint has a bearing on every aspect of your life both now and for eternity.

As you draw your study to a close today, look once more at the ways Paul so masterfully weaves together profound truths of who God is with invaluable instructions for the saint's daily life. Above all, be reminded that in Christ you have everything you need to live in the manner to which you've been called. "Grace be with all who have undying love for our Lord Jesus Christ" (Eph. 6:24).

48. Reflect on what Ephesians 6 reveals about:

God the Father	God the Son	God the Spirit

49. In your copy of the text on pp. 174–175, circle any abundance language you see. Look for words like *vast*, *full*, and *every*.

50. Consider how your understanding of the instructions to children/parents and slaves/masters has changed or grown now that you've studied these texts in light of the full letter to the Ephesians. Note key thoughts below.

◆ Children and parents

◆ Slaves and masters

51. Pick one text from Ephesians 1–2 that feels like an anchor passage for Ephesians 6:10-18, Paul's teaching on spiritual warfare and the armor of God. Write that passage in the space below.

52. Summarize in two to three sentences what you've learned from Ephesians about who God is (orthodoxy).

Summarize in two to three sentences what you've learned from Ephesians about putting your faith into practice (orthopraxy).

Spend some moments in quiet reflection as you let your thoughts linger on this New Testament book God has so graciously left us. "Now to him who is able to do above and beyond all that we ask or think according to the power that works in us—to him be glory in the church and in Christ Jesus to all generations, forever and ever. Amen" (Eph. 3:20-21).

WATCH

Watch the Session Seven video and take notes below.

TO ACCESS THE VIDEO SESSIONS, USE THE INSTRUCTIONS
IN THE BACK OF YOUR BIBLE STUDY BOOK.

DISCUSS

Discuss the following questions with your Bible study group. A more extensive leader guide is available for free download at **lifeway.com/ephesiansstudy.**

1. Which day of personal study had the most impact on you, and why? What lingering questions do you have?

2. How did what you heard on the video clarify, reinforce, or give new insight to what you studied this session?

3. How do the instructions in Ephesians 6:1-9 give you further understanding of how to imitate God in a wide range of relationships, from home to work to community?

4. We were reminded in the video that, in Christ and through the Spirit, we have everything we need to fight the spiritual battle we enter into daily. In light of this truth, encourage each other with ways you can boldly stand firm in your faith.

5. How do you want to live differently in the week to come because of what we've studied this week?

ENDNOTES

SESSION ONE

1. "Introduction to Ephesians," *Lifeway Women's Bible*, (Nashville: Holman Bible Publishers, 2022), 1708.

SESSION TWO

1. National Geographic Society. "Seven Wonders of the Ancient World." Accessed 2.6.24. https://education.nationalgeographic.org/resource/seven-wonders-ancient-world/.

2. John Stott, *The Message of Ephesians* (London, InterVarsity Press, 1979), 15.

3. Ephesians," in *CSB Study Bible Large Print*, 1870.

4. . John Newton, "Amazing Grace," *Hymnal.net*, accessed 2.6.24, https://www.hymnal.net/en/hymn/h/313.

5. The Westminster Divines, "The Westminster Shorter Catechism," *Ligonier Ministries*, accessed 2.6.24, https://www.ligonier.org/learn/articles/westminster-shorter-catechism.

6. "Ancient Seals or Signets," *Bible History*, accessed 2.6.24, https://bible-history.com/sketches/seals.

7. Tim Chester, *Into His Presence: Praying with the Puritans* (England, The Good Book Company, 2022), 53.

8. Stott, 36.

9. Frank Thielman, "Ephesians" (Grand Rapids: Baker Academics, 2010), 21.

SESSION THREE

1. Stott, 52

2. Stott, 53.

3. Stott, 66.

4. Stott, 79.

5. J. I. Packer, *Evangelism and the Sovereignty of God* (England: InterVarsity Press, 1961), 35-36.

SESSION FOUR

1. Butler, Trent C. Editor. Entry for 'Gentiles'. *Holman Bible Dictionary*. https://www.studylight.org/dictionaries/eng/hbd/g/gentiles.html. 1991.

2. Ibid.

3. Klyne Snodgrass, *The NIV Application Commentary: Ephesians* (Michigan, Zondervan, 1996), 165

4. Snodgrass, 165.

5. Stott, 102.

6. "What Is a Benediction?" *Ligonier Ministries*, accessed 2.6.24, https://www.ligonier.org/posts/what-benediction.

7. H.B. Charles Jr., "What is a Doxology?" *Ligonier Ministries*, YouTube, accessed 2.6.24, https://www.youtube.com/watch?v=zmddSKF_VBI&t=34s.

8. Ibid.

9. "Doxology," *Wilderness Wanderings*, Podcast, accessed 2.6.24, https://icrchww.libsyn.com/doxology.

SESSION FIVE

1. Douglas J. Moo, Craig L. Blomberg, Scott J. Hafemann, *NIVAC Bundle 7: Pauline Epistles* (United States, Zondervan, 2015).

2. Uncle Charlie, "The Fruit of the Spirit," *Genius.com*, accessed 2.6.24, https://genius.com/Uncle-charlie-fruit-of-the-spirit-lyrics.

3. Snodgrass, 196.

4. *Africa Bible Commentary* (United States, Zondervan, 2010), 1459.

5. John Stott, *Ephesians: Building a Community in Christ* (InterVaristy Press, 2020) 34.

6. Ludwig Bemelmens, *Madeline*, (London: Hippo, 1989).

7. Snodgrass, 254.

8. Jason Evans, "Overcoming Anger", *Sermons by Logos*, 2022.

9. Ibid.

SESSION SIX

1. "Who Divided the Bible into Chapters and Verses?," *Got Questions*, accessed 2.6.24, https://www.gotquestions.org/divided-Bible-chapters-verses.html.

2. Thielman, 322.

3. Anthony C. Thiselton, "The First Epistle to the Corinthians: A Commentary on the Greek Text," *New International Greek Testament Commentary* (Grand Rapids: W.B. Eerdmans, 2000), 439.

4. John R. W. Stott, *God's New Society: The Message of Ephesians*, The Bible Speaks Today (Downers Grove, IL: InterVarsity Press, 1979), 198.

5. Thielman, 339.

6. Hannah Anderson, *All That's Good: Recovering the Lost Art of Discernment*, (Moody Publishers, 2018), 26.

7. Calvin's Commentaries, "Ephesians 5:14", *BibleHub*, accessed 2.6.24, https://biblehub.com/commentaries/calvin/ephesians/5.htm.

8. Bell, Brian. "Commentary on Ephesians 1". *Bell's Commentary*, accessed 2.6.24, https://www.studylight.org/commentaries/eng/cbb/ephesians-1.html. 2017.

9. Hannah Anderson, *Humble Roots* (Moody Publishers, 2016), 91.

10. Thielman, 379.

11. Lynn Cohick, *Ephesians* (Lutterworth Press, 2013) 140.

12. Michelle Lee-Barnewall, *Neither Complementarian nor Egalitarian* (Baker Publishing Group, 2016), 284.

13. *Holman Bible Dictionary*. General Editor, Trent C. Butler, Ph.D. (Holman Bible Publishers, 2008).

SESSION SEVEN

1. Eugene Carpenter, "Exodus," ed. H. Wayne House and William D. Barrick, vol. 2, *Evangelical Exegetical Commentary* (Bellingham, WA: Lexham Press, 2012), 47.

2. Thielman, 399-400.

3. John R. W. Stott, *God's New Society: The Message of Ephesians, The Bible Speaks Today* (Downers Grove, IL: InterVarsity Press, 1979), 245.

4. Howard Thurman, *Jesus and the Disinherited* (United Kingdom: Beacon Press, 2022).

5. Cohick, 147.

6. Lisa Bowens, *African American Readings of Paul: Reception, Resistance, and Transformation* (Eerdmans, 2020) 117.

7. Ibid.

8. Ibid., 116.

9. Calvin, *Ephesians*, 169.

10. Thielman, 409.

11. Ibid., 410.

12. Lisa Bowens, *African American Readings of Paul*, (Grand Rapids: Eerdmans, 2020).

13. John R. W. Stott, *God's New Society: The Message of Ephesians, The Bible Speaks Today* (Downners Grove, IL: InterVarsity Press, 1979), 263.

14. Martin Lloyd-Jones, *The Christian Warfare: An Exposition of Ephesians 6:10-13*, (Baker Publishing Group, 2009) 154.

15. Ibid., 161.

16. David John Williams, *Paul's Metaphors: Their Context and Character*, (Hendrickson Publishers, 1999) 222.

17. Lloyd-Jones, 65.

18. John R. W. Stott, *God's New Society: The Message of Ephesians, The Bible Speaks Today* (Downers Grove, IL: InterVarsity Press, 1979), 232.

19. C. S. Lewis, *The Weight of Glory*, (Harper One, 2015).

20. Thielman.

Blessed is the God and Father of our Lord Jesus Christ, who has blessed us with every spiritual blessing in the heavens in Christ.

EPHESIANS 1:3

LOOKING FOR MORE? CHECK OUT THESE RESOURCES BY

Jackie Hill Perry

JUDE
7 Sessions

Dive into themes of being called, loved, and kept, and learn how to point others to Jesus in grace and truth as you study the book of Jude.

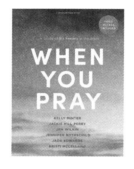

WHEN YOU PRAY
7 Sessions

Alongside Jackie and 5 other Bible teachers, study six prayers in the Bible that can renew and inspire your own.

HOLIER THAN THOU

Walk through Scripture, shaking the dust off of "holy" as we've come to know it, to reveal it for what it really is: good news.

GAY GIRL, GOOD GOD

Jackie Hill Perry shares her own story, offering practical tools that helped her in the process of finding wholeness.

UPON WAKING
60 DAYS

Dive into daily reflections on specific passages from Scripture to help you awaken to the God you were made for, the life you were made for, and the person you were made to be.

lifeway.com/jackiehillperry
To order by phone call 800.458.2772.

Lifeway women

Pricing and availability subject to change without notice.

Also Available from
Jasmine Holmes

AGES 6-10

Available where books are sold.

Get the most from your study.

Customize your Bible study time with a guided experience.

In this study you'll:

- Join Jackie Hill Perry, Jasmine Holmes, and Melissa Kruger in discussion-based video content, approximately 30-40 minutes each, that will inspire conversation in your own life
- Dive into themes of unity with Christ and unity with one another
- Comprehend the depths of God's love and discover the blessings of obedience to Christ

STUDYING ON YOUR OWN?

Watch Jackie Hill Perry, Jasmine Holmes, and Melissa Kruger's teaching sessions, available via redemption code for individual video-streaming access, printed in this Bible study book.

LEADING A GROUP?

Each group member will need an Ephesians Bible study book, which includes video access. Because all participants will have access to the video content, you can choose to watch the videos outside of your group meeting if desired. Or, if you're watching together and someone misses a group meeting, they'll have the flexibility to catch up! A DVD set is also available to purchase separately if desired.

Browse study formats, a free session sample, video clips, church promotional materials, and more at

lifeway.com/ephesiansstudy